The Crime Victim's Handbook

THE

Crime Victim's

HANDBOOK

Your Rights and Role in the
Criminal Justice System

David Austern

VIKING

VIKING
Viking Penguin Inc., 40 West 23rd Street,
New York, New York 10010, U.S.A.
Penguin Books Ltd, Harmondsworth,
Middlesex, England
Penguin Books Australia Ltd, Ringwood,
Victoria, Australia
Penguin Books Canada Limited, 2801 John Street,
Markham, Ontario, Canada L3R 1B4
Penguin Books (N.Z.) Ltd, 182–190 Wairau Road,
Auckland 10, New Zealand

First published in 1987 in simultaneous hardcover and paperback editions
by Viking Penguin Inc.
Published simultaneously in Canada

LIBRARY OF CONGRESS CATALOGING IN PUBLICATION DATA
Austern, David.
The crime victim's handbook.
1. Victims of crime—Legal status, laws, etc.—
United States—Popular works.   2. Reparation—United
States—Popular works.   I. Title.
KF9763.Z9A87   1987b   344.73'03288   86-40304
ISBN 0-670-80475-4   347.3043288

Printed in the United States of America by
R. R. Donnelley & Sons Company, Harrisonburg, Virginia
Set in Primer and Memphis
Designed by Vicky Hartman

For Marilyn, Elizabeth, and Phillip Austern,
who, on many long evenings and weekends of
research and writing, had to do without a husband
and a father, and for H. Thomas Austern,
the best lawyer I have ever known.

Acknowledgments

Scores of people contributed to this book—far too many to acknowledge here. I am grateful to all of them, but a few deserve special mention.

Ronald Goldfarb, my former law partner, convinced me I should write this book and offered both substantive and editorial comment. Gail Ross, with whom I also practiced law, reviewed early drafts and kept this project on schedule. Many victim advocates provided me with their judgment about what victims of crime would find most useful in a book of this kind. Karen Alexander and Joyce Dale, two experienced advocates, were particularly helpful.

The Sunny von Bulow National Victim Advocacy Center supplied the material from which I compiled the state listings for victim advocate and self-help groups.

Pat Mulcahy and Will Nixon of the Viking Penguin editorial staff gave me very important organizational and editorial help. If the explanations and descriptions of legal principles contained in this book are understandable by nonlawyers, it is because of their editoral skill and constant reminders to avoid legal jargon.

What sometimes appeared to be endless drafts were typed by many different people, but Regina Pruitt and Lisa Reynolds deserve special mention.

Most important of all, many chapters of this book were reviewed in draft form by crime victims. Five sexual assault victims, two spouse abuse victims, four child abuse victims—two of whom are survivors of incest and one of whom is also a spouse abuse victim—and two armed robbery victims read all or part of this book. Each gave substantive and editorial comment, which I invariably followed. All these victims have requested that I not mention their names, though I consider their contributions so significant that they deserve to be listed as coauthors. To them, my special thanks.

Contents

Introduction

During the past eight years, while I was representing crime victims and victim service providers, coauthoring several sets of training materials for victim advocates, and lecturing on the legal rights of crime victims, people sometimes asked, "But why the rights of crime victims? There are far more important legal issues in this country. What about the rights of the poor? How about the environment?"

Legal issues affecting the poor and the environment are important. So are many others. But like most people, I am influenced by personal experience, and I once had an experience involving a crime victim that forever changed my outlook on the subject.

In the spring of 1977, I taught a class on criminal procedure for correctional officers at the District of Columbia Jail. This was part of a nationwide program, funded in part by the federal government, to train correctional personnel about legal principles concerning the rights of defendants. The class met at the jail during the evening hours.

Like most jails, the District of Columbia Jail is located in a relatively unattractive part of the city. It is also located across the street from District of Columbia General Hospital where at that time injured crime victims were taken for medical attention. On a cold, rainy spring night, I left the jail after my class and ran to my car, which was parked in the Correctional Officers' parking lot. As I left the lot, my headlights swept the front entrance of the hospital. Standing at the entrance was a young woman who resembled one of my law students from the Georgetown University Law Center—except somehow this person looked different. I slowed down, and as I came abreast of the entrance I could see it was my law student. I stopped and asked her if she needed a ride.

The student—call her Judy—had been walking home from the law school a few hours earlier when she was accosted by a man with a gun who forced her into the garage of a nearby building. While in the garage, the man raped Judy, stole her purse, and beat her with the gun when she resisted both his sexual advances and the theft of her purse. Policemen in a passing cruiser heard Judy's screams, found the man pistol whipping his victim, and arrested the man on the spot.

In addition to the injuries caused by the sexual assault, Judy suffered lacerations to her face and neck—one of which required several stitches to close—a badly bruised muscle, a twisted ankle, and a broken tooth. She was taken in a police car to the hospital, where she was given a gynecological examination in a portion of the emergency room that was neither enclosed nor in any manner private. Although this examination was as much a procedure to establish that a sexual assault had occurred as it was to give medical attention to Judy, she was required to pay for it. In addition to there being a lack of privacy, the examination was performed by a person who appeared to Judy to be a non-

English-speaking physician, and in the presence of male police officers, one of whom told her during the examination that female law students take the place of more deserving male students.

Because virtually all of her clothes were covered with blood and thus were evidence of the crime, Judy's clothes were taken by the police and—despite the rain and the cold—she was given a paper dress and paper shoes to wear home. A robbery had been attempted, so her purse and all of its contents were seized by the police as evidence. She was given a dollar in order to take a bus across town to her apartment, and police and the hospital staff refused her request for a ride home or sufficient money to take a taxicab.

And that is how I saw Judy, standing in the rain in a paper dress and paper shoes, bandages on her face, without money or identification, without even the keys to her apartment—hopefully her roommate would be home—with firm instructions from the police to appear at the courthouse the next day to give a statement to the prosecutor, an official who might still decline to prosecute because of insufficient evidence.

Although Judy had taken courses in criminal law, criminal procedure, and evidence and had more knowledge about the criminal justice system than most victims of crime, she was more than a little appalled at her treatment as a crime victim. She knew there might be numerous court appearances if the case went to trial as well as the possibility—perhaps even the probability—that a defense investigator would inquire of her friends about her reputation, and that a defense attorney might cross-examine her at trial about prior acts of sexual intercourse. She knew from her law courses that the defendant, who was accused of both raping and robbing her, might be given, at no cost to him, the services of a lawyer, an investigator, a psychiatrist, and other professionals. She knew the United States Constitution guaranteed certain rights to the defendant in a criminal case. Although Judy had never thought about it before, she now realized the same Constitution guaranteed virtually no rights to a crime victim—or at least at that time the courts had so interpreted the Constitution.

But what she did not know was the way the criminal justice system at that time treated many victims of crime from the very moment the crime was reported.

"The rape and beating were bad enough," Judy said, "but the way I was treated after that was even worse. I knew they could tear me apart in court, but I sure didn't know about the rest—they took my clothes, my money, my keys, my credit cards, they examined me in public, they insulted me, and then they billed me. Well, anyway, they didn't take my law books because fortunately I didn't have them with me." Would she ever report a crime in the future? She thought about that for several long minutes and then, apparently for the first time since she had been victimized by the accused and by the criminal justice system, Judy cried. I stopped the car and she leaned against my shoulder for a while.

"You know," she said after a few minutes, "next time I won't even scream. Somebody might hear me and call the police."

Judy's roommate was home and, as luck would have it, was a psychiatric nurse who worked at another hospital. At that time there was no counseling at District of Columbia General Hospital for sexual assault victims—that, too, has changed—and the roommate's professional training was of great assistance.

The three of us talked for a while, and then I continued on my way home thinking as I drove about the hundreds of crime victims I had dealt with in my nearly nine years as a prosecutor, and how very little I knew about the victims or about how the crime they had experienced might have changed their lives. I was so busy interviewing the victims, presenting the case in court, or supervising other lawyers that I never stepped back and looked at what the victim was going through. I remembered several years earlier when a robbery victim had commented to me after a trial that in all of his contacts with police, prosecutors, and court personnel, nobody had asked him how he felt about the case. And I remembered my colleagues and I chuckling at lunch about the victim's comment. Who really cared? After all, how a crime victim felt was of no help in getting a conviction.

In short, prior to the mid-1970s, few if any people in this country paid much attention to crime victims. It was almost as if the entire criminal justice system focused so intensely on the rights of the accused that there was no time or attention left for the victim. In many respects, that has changed. This book is about some of those changes.

Although it describes legal rights, this book is intended for readers who are not lawyers. There are no footnotes, and case citations are not used. Lawyers may use the book for basic research, but it was never intended that this be a legal text or treatise.

The chapters that follow address some of the legal rights of victims of crime. Chapter 1 describes the criminal justice system and its relationship to victims. Some years ago, in referring to the criminal justice system's treatment of victims, a prosecutor described the process as "the criminal injustice system." While times have changed and the treatment of crime victims has improved, elements of injustice do remain, particularly for those victims unfamiliar with their rights.

Chapters 2 and 3 describe third-party litigation in which crime victims file lawsuit against third parties—not the person who actually committed the crime, but someone else—on the grounds that the third party's negligent conduct contributed to the crime and to the injury to the victim. Chapter 2 describes third-party litigation against government agencies or their representatives such as the police, corrections officers, and hospitals, while Chapter 3 describes third-party litigation against private parties or institutions such as landlords, hotels, business establishments, and transportation companies. Third-party litigation has increased dramatically during the past few years. Despite what you may have read or heard, the number of civil cases filed in state and federal courts has not increased, but the number of third-party cases has, perhaps because more victims are aware that they may be able to recover their losses from people whose conduct may have led to a commission of the crime.

The next three chapters describe specific types of crimes and certain legal rights unique to their victims. Chapter 4 addresses the legal issues affecting the rights of the most frequent crime victims—children, who are also undoubtedly the most underreported victims. Crimes against children present unique procedural problems, such as when and under what circumstances the children should be permitted to testify in court. Chapter 5 describes spouse abuse, another underreported crime, and the recently enacted legislation that in many cases can put a stop to the cycle of violence present in many families. Frequently, these cases are not treated as a crime by law-enforcement officials and instead are referred to Family Court, which is inappropriate because it relegates to the civil justice system something more properly resolved by the criminal justice system. Chapter 6 presents the legal rights of victims of sexual assault. Like the law student, Judy, these victims have special problems because of the highly emotional and intimate nature of the crime. For them, sexual assault is a crime like no other, but the criminal justice system does not always treat it as such.

Chapter 7 describes victim compensation and restitution, two programs through which victims sometimes receive money from a state agency or from the accused following a court order. Chapter 8 describes when and under what circumstances a person may use self-defense—including deadly weapons—to avoid becoming a victim of crime.

Finally, Chapter 9 describes the growth and development of victim service agencies and organizations. Twenty years ago there were no such agencies, but today there are quite literally thousands of agencies that offer advice and comfort to crime victims.

During the one hundred or more meetings at which I have spoken about victims' rights, I have asked the audience how many of them have been victims or have family members who have so suffered. Typically, between 80 and 90 percent of the audience answers affirmatively. But when I ask how many of them know their rights as crime victims, less than 10 percent do. As noted in Chapter 9, crime victim advocates give advice to victims and have significantly advanced their rights in recent years. But these advocates cannot counsel every crime victim, for there are too few advocates and too many victims. In fact, the best crime victim advocate is the victim who knows his or her rights and will seek to exercise them. This book is intended to help such people and to enlist their aid as advocates for all crime victims.

The Crime Victim's Handbook

·1·

The Criminal Justice System and Crime Victims

Fifty-seven million Americans will be the victims of crime this year. Some will not report the crime, but they will all experience the economic loss, the physical pain, and the emotional upset that victimization can cause. It is hard to find a home in which someone has not been the victim of a crime, and that is no small wonder when you consider that almost two crimes are committed every second.

In the minute or so it will take you to read this page and the next, thirteen homes will be burglarized, nine people will be assaulted, and at least two people will be seriously injured as the result of a criminal act. In the same minute, at least one child will be physically abused.

These statistics come from the United States Department of Justice, but there are more such statistics, and they are even worse. We seem to count crime much better than we prevent it or solve it. For instance, we know that on the average, twenty women are raped every hour—twenty-four hours a day, seven days a week, Saturdays, Sundays, and holidays included—over 175,000 a year. Sadly, many experts believe that figure is far below the number of rapes that actually occur. Generally, we know that sexual assault of women, men, children, and the elderly is an underreported crime. Victims of these crimes are reluctant to complain to the police or to anyone else. One national study reported that fewer than 20 percent of the women who are sexually assaulted report the crime to a law enforcement agency. If that is true, one woman is sexually assaulted every thirty-six seconds. And that does not take into account sexually assaulted and molested children, a crime all experts agree is even more underreported than the sexual assault of women.

Some crimes, however, are almost always reported or at least detected. Although occasionally you read about missing persons whose bodies are discovered in a mass grave, most homicides are reported to the police soon after they occur. These reports keep the police busy. Fifty-five people are murdered every day, over twenty thousand a year. Even at the height of the Vietnam War, fewer Americans lost their lives in that conflict each year than as the result of a homicide at home. Of course, twenty thousand people murdered every year leave behind hundreds of thousands of children, spouses, parents, close friends, and countless others whose lives are forever altered by the loss.

These statistics do not include the thousands of people who lose their lives every year as the result of automobile accidents involving negligence, or industrial accidents, or other incidents in which a person is killed because of the act of another. Our legal system does not define the killing of another as a homicide unless the person responsible for the death intended to kill the victim, or at least acted so recklessly that death was foreseeable. That definition does *not* include negligent acts like driving too fast, and in most states it does not even include driving too fast after drinking an entire bottle of Scotch. Although there are many homicide victims, there would be even more but for our narrow definition.

The cost in human lives and suffering is staggering, but so is the loss in dollars. We will lose about $75,000,000,000—that's not a misprint, it's $75 *billion*—to crime this year. That figure does not include the over $25 billion the United States will spend this year fighting crime. When next you hear that the federal government or a unit of local government is unable to balance its budget, ask yourself whether the budget could be balanced if we neither lost nor spent $100 billion a year because of crime. In a time of multibillion-dollar budgets at the federal level and in some states, it might be useful to remember that this $100 billion is more than the annual budget for one hundred and four of the one hundred and fifty-six *countries* in the world.

Of course, if this were a book about the economics of crime—and it is not—we could discuss the real "cost" of crime in other ways as well. Chapters would be devoted to an analysis of what you and I pay for merchandise over and above the fair market price because the store owner loses money to shoplifting; what we all pay for insurance because of losses due to criminal acts which are paid to victims by insurance companies; and what the cost to society is when productive, useful people can no longer work because they were crime victims. All of these are costs, and they could probably be quantified, but for a description of victims' legal rights, that kind of dollar-by-dollar counting is unnecessary. It's also a little cold and heartless, and while the law may be cold and heartless, it's not nearly as bad as a pure numbers game.

In his book *The Ages of American Law,* Professor Grant Gilmore observed:

> In heaven, there will be no law and the lion will lie down with the lamb. . . . In hell, there will be nothing but law, and due process will be meticulously observed.

Although Professor Gilmore was not the first to make such an observation, he did fairly summarize the opinion held by many, particularly applied to the criminal justice system. Another commentator has observed that the American criminal justice system is concerned only with process and not with guilt and innocence, or even right and wrong. Unfortunately, this meticulous concern with due process has led to the victim of crime becoming the forgotten participant in the criminal justice system.

That was not always true. Prior to the emergence of feudal society, it was up to the victim of a criminal act to arrest, prosecute, and perhaps even execute the offender. As feudal lords began to offer protection to vassals, however, the theory of social contract emerged and was pushed and shaped into a meaningful form by Locke, Rousseau, and others. In its basic text, social contract theory calls for individuals to surrender some of their rights to society in exchange for society's promise to protect the individual. It became the duty of society—usually in the form of a government institution—to protect the individual, to arrest a person who unlawfully attacked a victim, to prosecute the offender, and to punish the person convicted. The victim of crime, in turn, gave up these rights.

However, even though society provided some services, victims of crime did retain limited rights to assist or even take the place of a government agency. This limited right of assistance or substitution varied from time to time and place to place. For instance, in England during the seventeenth and eighteenth centuries, private prosecutions, whereby the individual could charge and prosecute the offender, were commonplace. It is not surprising, therefore, to discover that in the original thirteen American colonies, private prosecution was permitted and was the customary means of bringing an accused person before the courts.

Police protection was slow to develop. There were few if any organized police forces in any society prior to the eighteenth century. The military authorities or the victim performed the now traditional police functions of prevention and detection of crime. As police forces became a part of the government, the victim no longer had to apprehend the offender. Except as described below, the victim also had no power to arrest an individual the police chose not to arrest. As with prosecution, the assumption by the government of the policing responsibility may have protected the victim, but it also removed from the victim the power to arrest.

Today we accept the government's role to provide the physical requirements and personal services needed to operate a criminal justice system. As a consequence, the victim—until very recently—has had little or no say about whether a person would be arrested, prosecuted, or punished. In short, the victim of crime has become only a witness in the criminal justice system.

During the past decade, individuals, institutions (both public and private), and legal scholars have examined the role of the crime victim. Almost without exception, they have concluded that changes are needed, that the role of the crime victim has been ill defined and even worse, ignored. Until very recently, little or no thought has been given to the appropriate role for the victim, and most criminal justice practitioners have failed even to think about the crime victim's needs. That is changing—slowly.

The Criminal "Injustice System": A Hypothetical Case

Following a case through the criminal "injustice" system as a victim can be discouraging. Perhaps you've already had the misfortune of being a crime victim and becoming involved with police, prosecutors, and other criminal justice practitioners.

Let's follow a hypothetical case through the system to see what most usually happens. A hypothetical case is the most useful descriptive tool because individual cases inevitably differ.

Assume you are walking near your home during the early evening hours. Suddenly a car stops next to you, a man with a gun jumps from the car and tells you to give him your money. You hand over your wallet, which contains cash, credit cards, and other identification, including your driver's license. Then he hits you in the face with the barrel of the gun, and, as you fall to the ground, he returns to his car and drives away. A neighbor, who has seen the incident, calls the police, reports the license number of the car, and comes to your aid.

A few minutes later, while your neighbor is helping you stop the bleeding from the gash in your cheek, the police arrive with a man in handcuffs. You immediately identify him as the person who assaulted and robbed you. The man is arrested. If he has your cash and credit cards, they will be returned to you after they are photographed by the police, at least in most jurisdictions. The police will offer to take you to a hospital for medical attention. Even if you refuse, the police may wish to photograph you in order to present evidence of the assault to a jury.

In some but not all jurisdictions there will be a victim/witness office in the local prosecutor's office to assist you through the criminal justice system and to explain your rights and responsibilities as a victim. In some places, however, you will have to figure them out for yourself.

Traditionally, police perform two functions, prevention and detection of crime. In detection, the police investigate allegations of criminal conduct and, if the allegations are correct and an offender can be identified, they make an arrest. At least that's the way it's supposed to work. In the real world, however, police rarely perform in this manner.

The investigation usually follows a report to the police that a crime has been committed. Your neighbor's call to the police is an example. Occasionally the police will witness a crime, and even more occasionally a police officer will be the victim of a crime. However, private citizens' reports to the police are by far the largest source of information about criminal activity.

The police are not required to investigate every reported crime, and, in fact, do not. The decision about which crimes to investigate and which to ignore is left to their discretion. Of course, the police cannot investigate all reported crimes, nor can they investigate all serious crimes immediately after the report is made.

For instance, if at the time your neighbor called the police the available officers on duty were answering other calls, the investigation of your robbery would have been delayed. The volume of reported crimes, and the fact that many crimes are reported during the same hours of the same days—particularly Friday and Saturday nights—requires that the police defer some investigations in favor of more serious ones.

Almost without exception, the courts have refused to interfere with this exercise of discretion. In one case, a court required the Federal Bureau of Investigation to investigate the alleged criminal violation of certain civil rights statutes, but that was a decision based on political and racial constitutionally mandated protections. Other courts have ordered local police investigations where it appeared the decision not to investigate was based on the race or religion of the victim. However, except where racial or religious prejudice form the basis for the decision not to investigate, courts do not order the police to investigate a reported crime.

Of course, if the police do not investigate a crime, they are unlikely to be in a position to arrest the perpetrator. But assuming an investigation takes place, or assuming the perpetrator is otherwise identified, the police are not required to make an arrest. The decision to arrest is also within the discretion of the police.

In many states, police may (but not must) arrest for any felony, but can (but not must) arrest only for misdemeanors committed in their presence. A misdemeanor is usually defined as a crime for which the perpetrator can be sentenced to prison for a maximum term of less than one year, while a felony is a crime carrying a sentence of more than one year. A few states impose a criminal penalty on police officers who fail to arrest for a crime committed in their presence, but research does not disclose a case of a police officer actually being prosecuted for violating such a statute. For misdemeanors not committed in their presence, most states require an officer to obtain a warrant in order to make an arrest.

Suppose the police refuse to investigate your robbery, or suppose they identify the person who committed the crime, but refuse to arrest him. What can you do? Practically nothing. The courts have determined that a private citizen may not sue the police to force them to arrest a person who committed a crime. Although some public officials can be sued to force them to take action where they are required by law to perform a particular act, the police have the discretion not to investigate or arrest, and thus the courts will not force them to perform these discretionary acts. As noted in Chapter 3, a victim cannot ordinarily recover civil damages from the police based on their failure to make an arrest. More importantly, the fact that a victim wanted the perpetrator arrested rarely if ever is cited as a reason by the police to make an arrest. Simply stated, the victim's wishes are unimportant.

Can the victim of crime make a "citizen's arrest"? Usually a citizen's arrest is permissible where the crime is committed in the citizen's presence. However, in addition to the obvious prudence a citizen should exercise in arresting the perpetrator of a crime—particularly when the person being arrested is armed or is just plain bigger—a victim should remember that he or she is liable for false arrest if the wrong person is arrested.

One of the reasons so many victims refuse to report crimes is a large and measurable dissatisfaction with the criminal justice system. The police are only one component of this system, but they are the most visible, and they have the most frequent contact with crime victims. When a victim finds the police unresponsive, or responsive but uncooperative, or just plain uninterested in the victim's needs, a further erosion of the criminal justice system takes place. Such victims are unlikely to report subsequent criminal acts that take place against them or others.

The single most important prerequisite to effective law enforcement is the willingness of crime victims to cooperate. Where victims are unwilling or even reluctant to assist law enforcement personnel, police work is more difficult and less productive, conviction rates go down, and crime increases. One recent study found that of every one hundred felonies committed in this country, only thirty-three are reported to the police. Only ten result in an arrest, and only three result in a conviction.

Requiring the police to investigate and, where possible, arrest in every case would be impossible, inappropriate, and perhaps even silly. But requiring the police to listen to victims, help victims, and express concern for them is not silly. It is necessary.

Prosecution

Assume the arrest of the person who assaulted you: Must the prosecutor bring the case to court? Again, the answer is no.

Prosecutors decline to prosecute for a number of reasons. First, some arrests are made for acts that are simply not crimes. Stated differently, the police observe or hear about the conduct of an accused and make an arrest, but that conduct, when compared to the criminal statute in question, is found not to be a violation of law.

Second, some arrests are made for the violation of a criminal statute but, in the prosecutor's judgment, were made with less than probable cause, i.e., the police should not have made the arrest. This is the case if an improper search of the accused is made at the time of the arrest. Thus if that search revealed the accused was carrying narcotics or a weapon, the case could not proceed to court because the narcotics or the weapon could not be used in evidence. Similarly, if the only evidence in the case is a confession, but one which was made in violation of the accused's right to remain silent, the case could not proceed to court because the confession would be inadmissible.

Third, prosecutors sometimes reject cases because they lack what is referred to as "prosecutive merit," which often means the prosecutor does not believe the case will result in a conviction. For instance, as noted in Chapter 5, some prosecutors refuse to prosecute where a husband is accused of assaulting his wife because they believe a jury will not vote to convict in such cases. Some prosecutors believe the possession of a small amount of drugs also lacks prosecutive merit. Finally, there are some prosecutors and some jurisdictions that employ first offender treatment programs through which people accused of minor offenses can devote time to community service; if they successfully complete the service, the prosecutor will dismiss pending charges. Frequently, when a minor case lacks prosecutive merit, the prosecutor offers first-offender treatment to the accused.

Some prosecutors reject cases for political reasons. Essentially, cases that will not lead to a conviction are rejected because elected prosecutors—the overwhelming majority—must run for reelection against their trial record, and a prosecutor who has a low conviction rate may be defeated by a political opponent critical of the incumbent's conviction rate. Such a prosecutor usually accepts for prosecution cases that will result in a conviction, and usually rejects cases that will result in an acquittal. In addition, there are "political" cases of a more traditional nature: as an elected official, the prudent prosecutor does not deliberately offend the political power structure in the election district, which may result in some cases that should be prosecuted being dismissed. Fortunately, few prosecutors are motivated by purely political considerations when determining which cases to prosecute.

In some areas, a crime victim can employ a lawyer to act as a "private" prosecutor to charge a person with a criminal act and bring the case to court. However, in many of these areas the private prosecutor must act under the control and authority of the elected or appointed prosecutor, and the private prosecutor may only bring the case to court if the elected prosecutor agrees.

In some states a warrant for arrest may be issued on the complaint of a private citizen without the assistance or the concurrence of the police or prosecutor. However, even in areas where this is true, the accused may not be tried in court without the permission of the local prosecutor.

On a number of occasions, crime victims have sued

prosecutors to force them to prosecute. However, without exception, the courts have held that the decision to prosecute—or not to prosecute—is not reviewable by the courts. Even the Supreme Court has stated that a crime victim could not ask the courts to overrule or even question the policies of the prosecutor.

The Prosecution Function: The Victim's
Rights When the Accused Is Tried in Court

Among the most dramatic changes in the criminal justice system's recognition of the needs of victims has been the establishment in hundreds of local prosecutors' offices of victim/witness assistance units. In 1970, there were practically no such units; today there are almost three hundred. At the end of this chapter is a list with at least one such unit for almost every state.

Victim/witness assistance units were established to provide specific service to victims and witnesses of crimes and to refer such people to other agencies that provide other victim services. The units perform a number of important functions.

First and perhaps most important of all, they give victims a single contact within the prosecutor's office with whom to confer. Typically, in large urban prosecutor's offices, cases are moved from one prosecutor to another as the case progresses through the system. In addition, personnel changes lead to cases being handled by many different lawyers assigned by the prosecutor. As a result, the victim may have to talk to many different prosecutors before the case is concluded, but the victim/witness unit remains a contact for information.

If you are a victim you will almost certainly want to know what is happening to the case. Instead of speaking to different prosecutors—many of whom are in court much of the day and hard to reach by telephone—you can call the victim/witness assistance unit for information. Some units have personnel who can explain to a victim the different stages of a court case, and who can tell a victim when and where they will be needed. Although many victims have some knowledge of the criminal justice system, the technicalities can be so bewildering that some explanation is required in almost every case. And many victim/witness assistance units have personnel who are not under the intense pressure to dispose of a large number of cases, as assistant district attorneys usually are, and who therefore are able to be more compassionate and understanding.

Sometimes both victims and witnesses are threatened by persons accused of crimes. Several years ago, the American Bar Association held public hearings concerning this matter and discovered victim and witness intimidation to be far more pervasive than many people thought. A victim/witness assistance unit can work with other prosecution personnel and the police to make sure victims and others who testify remain free of intimidation. In some states, victims and witnesses receive written notice—according to state statute—of their right to request protection from intimidation, although in other states written notice is given only to victims of certain crimes, or is not given at all.

The criminal justice system's concern for process almost inevitably results in frequent court appearances for every criminal case. It is not uncommon for a case that proceeds to trial to involve over ten court dates. In addition, the trial may not occur on the scheduled date. As a result, victims and witnesses are frequently called to court, asked to be available on certain dates, but not consulted as to whether the scheduled court date is convenient. Many victim/witness assistance units clear dates in advance with the victims before a prosecutor agrees in court to a new one. Even where this is not done, these units notify victims as soon as possible of when the next continued date is scheduled.

Crime victims who are forced to make one or more court appearances sometimes suffer loss of wages or unfavorable employer comments. Frequently, the victim/witness assistance unit can intercede with an employer and explain the importance of the victim's court appearances. Occasionally this unit can explain to a victim's creditors the extent of the victim's losses as a result of the criminal act. The creditors may be asked to forego repayment until the victim has had the opportunity to recover—both physically and economically—from the effects of the crime.

Victim/witness assistance units and prosecution rules in some states have also produced a dramatic change in the rights of victims. For instance, in some states the victim's opinion about the defendant's right to bail at the first court appearance must be told to the judge by the prosecutor, or by the victim. In other states the prosecutor or another official must inform the victim of the outcome of the case, something of particular importance because the vast majority of criminal cases are disposed of through guilty pleas and (except as noted below), crime victims are not usually consulted about the acceptance of such pleas.

Plea bargaining is the process in which a defense attorney and a prosecutor meet to determine whether the case can be disposed of without trial. Typically, the parties agree that the defendant will plead guilty to fewer crimes and less serious crimes than the ones with which he or she is charged.

In a few jurisdictions, plea bargaining is not permitted at all. In others, the prosecutor cannot plea bargain without first consulting the victim to discover the victim's opinion on what would be an appropriate plea. And in at least one jurisdiction, an assistant prosecutor may not accept a plea of guilty to any crime other than the crime charged in the criminal complaint without the approval of the victim. In that jurisdiction, the district attorney can accept the guilty plea that the assistant cannot, but the district attorney cannot overrule the victim unless the district attorney concludes the victim is unreasonable.

The next stage in the criminal justice process is sentencing. As described in Chapter 7, many jurisdictions use victim impact statements through which the sentencing judge can learn what happened to the victim as a result of the crime. Such a statement is useful in determining if incarceration for the defendant is appropriate, and if restitution should be ordered. But in addition to the victim impact statement, many jurisdictions require that the victim be notified as to when and where the defendant will be sentenced so the victim can be present. And some jurisdictions require the sentencing judge to permit the victim to address the court to explain his or her views with respect to the appropriate sentence.

Victim testimony is almost always needed to prove the defendant committed the crime. However, at both the bail and sentencing stage, victim appearance in court is relatively new. It has created at least one procedural difficulty and has resulted in a curious phenomenon. In some states the victim is entitled to be present at a bail hearing, and in many states a victim must be notified if the defendant is released before the trial. However, unless the defendant is arrested at the scene of the crime or very shortly thereafter, the victim will not be present at the arrest. Because in all jurisdictions there must be a bail hearing very shortly after the arrest—in fact, the same day except for weekend arrests—some victims will not be available to come to court for the bail hearing. It also may be difficult to notify the victim that an arrest has been made in the short period between arrest and bail hearing, and if the defendant is released, it may be difficult to notify the victim about the defendant's status. That is particularly true when there's been a long period between the crime and the arrest.

All of these difficulties may prevent the victim from appearing at the bail hearing even in those states where it is permitted.

Although in some states victims have the right to be present or to speak at sentencing, many victims are reluctant to do so. In Nebraska a sentencing court must consider written statements by victims. Where there are none, the official conducting the presentence investigation must certify that he has attempted to contact the victim. If the victim is contacted, oral statements by the victim must be reduced to writing by the official. Despite this, during a 1985 meeting of Nebraska trial judges, very few reported ever having a victim come to court to make an oral statement, and less than 20 percent of the judges had received a written statement from a victim. Almost one-half the judges who had a case in which the victim came to court reported that the victim requested the court to be lenient with the defendant, not harsh.

In addition to notifying the victim about the date of the sentencing, victim/witness assistance units can help victims recover their stolen property needed as evidence; in some states the law requires that the property be promptly returned to the victim after it is photographed. They can also help victims receive witness fees, which in most states are very low, and they can refer victims with special needs—such as the elderly or parents of very young victims—to trained professionals.

Some states have additional after-sentencing victims' rights. In some jurisdictions, victims are permitted to express their views at parole hearings, and the parole boards are required to consider these statements when reviewing parole determinations. In addition, in some states, a victim must be notified when the person responsible for a criminal act is released on parole or has completed his sentence. If the defendant escapes from prison, the victim must also be notified. However, if the victim has moved since the time of the sentencing, problems can arise. For example, Illinois is one of those states that requires notification of victims when an offender is scheduled to appear before the parole board. The Illinois parole board reports that over 50 percent of its letter notifications are returned because the victim has moved and there is no available forwarding address.

Where Does Crime Occur?

A person is less likely to become a victim of a crime in some parts of the country than in others. Generally, you are safer in a rural setting than in an urban one and safer in some states than in others. Not surprisingly, those states with the highest crime rates have typically (but not always) been the first to address the legal rights of crime victims. Sadly there are still some states with high crime rates— and some cities and counties with staggering crime rates— that have been reluctant to provide legal rights and remedies to crime victims, preferring instead to expand the rights of the accused.

But the "geography" of victimization is more than looking at a map to determine where victims are located. Surprisingly, your legal rights as a crime victim may be determined not by what happened to you, not by considering your injuries or losses, but by where the crime occurred. There are two reasons for this.

First, state and local laws are not the same with respect to the legal rights of crime victims. For instance, in some states there is victim compensation—the state will compensate you for your injuries—for many victims of crime, including nonresidents. This compensation includes awards for pain and suffering as well as awards for physical injury, emotional distress, and lost wages. (See Chapter 7.) In other states, however, there is no victim compensation, and the judges of the state courts are reluctant even to order the convicted offender to pay the victim for the loss suffered in those cases in which the convicted offender could do so.

In some states there are rape shield laws (as discussed in Chapter 6) that protect a sexual assault victim from being cross-examined at trial (except in a few instances) about any prior acts of sexual intercourse. But in others there are no such laws, and the state courts both welcome and expect defense attorneys to attempt to embarrass a victim who has accused someone of sexual assault. In short, the laws of the state in which you become a crime victim will be far more important in determining your legal rights than the injury you suffered.

More troubling, within each state your relationship to the person who committed the crime against you is of crucial importance in determining your legal rights. For instance, despite rhetoric by politicians seeking election that citizens should be safe from crime on the streets, the sad fact is that you have a far greater chance of becoming a crime victim in your own home than any other place. Even more troubling, for the violent crimes of murder, sexual abuse, child abuse, and assault, you are more likely to be victimized by a relative than by a stranger. In many states, you can receive victim compensation, but not if you were victimized by a member of your own family. In others you can accuse someone of rape and that person will be arrested and prosecuted, but not if the accused is your spouse. Usually, a person will be prosecuted if he assaults a child, but less frequently if the offender is a parent. It is even possible— and this has actually happened—that a state will deny victim compensation to children who become technical orphans because their mother is murdered by their father, who then is sentenced to life imprisonment, because the children became victims due to an intrafamily offense. One state court ruled that a child who suffered emotional distress because she witnessed her father kill her mother (he then tried to kill the child) could not recover damages because the father had "parental immunity."

In short, there is a Catch-22 to your legal rights as a crime victim: you are more likely to be victimized by a family member than by a stranger. Yet even those states that provide significant legal rights and remedies to crime victims tend to narrow such rights—or eliminate them altogether—when your assailant is a member of your family.

Who Are the Victims?

There was a time in this country, not long ago, when criminal justice experts instructed us that most victims of crime came from the lower economic, poorly educated, and disadvantaged part of society. However, we know today that crime—even violent crime—touches all of us, and the legal rights of victims are for all victims, not just those who are poor. For instance, the *second most likely* victim of spouse abuse is the spouse of someone with a postcollege degree; if you're married to a lawyer, doctor, professor, etc., you're more likely to become the victim of spouse abuse than if you're married to someone who had no formal education after high school. Although statistics on unreported crime are very difficult to analyze, it appears that the better-educated, wealthy person is four times *less likely* to report domestic violence than the poorly educated spouse who is victimized. At least some experts believe similar statistics apply to child abuse, that is, the more affluent the family, the less likely it is that the abuse will be detected or reported.

However, there appears to be a relationship between the economic resources of a victim and how well that victim can exercise his or her legal rights. For instance, Chapters 2 and 3 describe the legal rights of a crime victim to sue a third person—but not the offender—who is at least partially responsible for the victimization. Lawsuits against hotels by guests who are assaulted in the hotel are an example. But access to the courts, and the ability to employ an attorney who will argue for your legal rights, can be an expensive proposition. Knowledge about the legal rights available to crime victims is bound to be more readily available to better-educated victims.

As discussed more fully in Chapter 7, victim compensation and restitution programs tend to favor people without insurance. Yet, while a wealthy person with casualty, health, or property insurance, or an income level such that tax deductions for losses are available, is unlikely to receive victim compensation, he is likely to be better off even without compensation than a victim whose economic status makes him eligible for compensation. In the event of a loss, insurance is almost always a better protection than victim compensation, because some compensation programs have narrow eligibility criteria and low maximum awards.

Although we are all likely to become victims of crime, those of us who can afford the loss the least are the most likely to be uninformed about victims' rights and the most likely to be unable to take advantage of the existing legal remedies. In a country that prides itself on having an "equal protection" criminal justice system for the accused—everyone accused of crime has the same rights—it is unfortunate that equal protection is not a right of crime victims as well.

The criminal justice system also provides a basis for determining what crime is charged, but that basis is legally and morally troubling. For instance, when the crime committed is a theft, the question of whether you are the victim of a felony, which carries a sentence of more than one year, or a misdemeanor—less than a year—almost always depends on the value of the thing stolen, not on the cost of replacing it. Nor is the law concerned with whether the victim lost something of tremendous sentimental worth but little monetary value. If the family heirloom stolen is worth only $50—even though your grandparents gave it to your parents who gave it to you—you are the victim of a misdemeanor.

Even worse, what actually happens to you as the victim of a crime may be less important in determining the seriousness of the crime than what the offender intended to do. For instance, in one study of elderly women who were the victims of purse snatching in a midwestern city, when and if caught the offenders were charged with relatively minor crimes because the victims were not seriously hurt at the time of the purse snatching. However, within one year of the purse snatching, almost one-half of all of the victims had died. Why? For some it may have been the emotional shock. For others, it may have been the trauma associated with moving to new living quarters caused by losing money in the purse snatching. Some victims probably would have died anyway because all of the victims studied were elderly. However, no offender was charged with murder. It would have been extremely difficult—perhaps even impossible—for the prosecutor to have proven at a trial that the purse snatching was the cause of death. Thus what actually happened to the victim of the crime became less important—at least in the eyes of the law—than what the offender intended to do.

When classifying crimes, the law also tends to ignore the ability of the victim to withstand the loss of property or the physical injury. For instance, an elderly person, living alone on a fixed income, cannot easily replace a stolen television set. The stolen property may have been the only form of entertainment the victim could afford, and might even have been the only communication the victim had with the outside world. In contrast, some people can easily replace a dozen stolen television sets; they may even have insurance that will assist them to do so. But the law treats both victims the same; they have been the victim of a burglary and a larceny. Although we treat those accused of crimes equally— a defendant in a criminal case who is poor, emotionally disturbed, or physically injured is treated the same as an affluent, healthy person—such equality is nonexistent when it comes to providing legal rights to crime victims.

The Federal Government and the Crime Victim

Local crime is a local problem. Although there are federal crimes such as tax fraud, narcotics violations, and interstate transportation of stolen property, crimes of violence such as murder, assault, and rape are prosecuted under local law and are investigated by local police. Except for the assault or murder of a federal employee or a crime of violence committed on federal property, local crimes of violence remain local for all purposes. Unlike many countries, we have neither a national police force nor a national district attorney to investigate and prosecute all crimes.

As a result, until very recently, the federal government has been inactive in addressing the rights of violent crime victims. But in 1980, President-Elect Ronald Reagan created a Victims of Crime Task Force, and subsequently a Presidential Commission of Victims of Crime. As described in Chapter 9, a second presidential commission investigated domestic violence. In 1982, Congress passed the Victim/ Witness Protection Act, but this act was applicable only to victims and witnesses appearing in federal courts. After numerous attempts to convince Congress to pass a federal victim compensation law had failed, such a law was passed finally in 1984.

An example of the federal government's inattention to

the problems of crime victims can be found in the fact that between 1968 and 1980, the Law Enforcement Assistance Administration, a government grant agency, awarded approximately $7.5 billion in criminal justice grants. Less than 1 percent of the money—less than $50 million—was directed to help victims of crime. In the same period, over $1 billion was awarded to improve services for and conditions of persons convicted of commiting crime.

REPRESENTATIVE VICTIM/WITNESS ASSISTANCE UNITS BY STATE

Victim/Witness Assistance Unit
District Attorney's Office
601 Courthouse
Birmingham, AL 35263
(205) 325-5272

Victim/Witness Assistance
Program
Pouch KT
Juneau, AK 99811
(907) 465-3678

Victim/Witness Program
4th Floor
101 W. Jefferson Ave.
Phoenix, AZ 85003
(602) 262-8522

Victim/Witness Program
City Court House, #301
Fort Smith, AR 72901
(501) 783-8976

Victim/Witness Assistance
Program
1600 City Hall E.
200 N. Main
Los Angeles, CA 90012
(213) 485-6979

Victim Witness Assistance
District Attorney's Office
800 Bryant St.
San Francisco, CA 94103
(415) 552-6550

Victim Witness Assistance
924 W. Colfax
Denver, CO 80204
(303) 575-5822

Victim/Witness Program
State's Attorney's Office
95 Washington St.
Hartford, CT 06106
(203) 366-3190

Victim/Witness Assistance
Program
Delaware Department of Justice
820 N. French St.
Wilmington, DE 19801
(302) 571-2599

Victim/Witness Assistance Unit
U.S. Attorney's Office
500 Indiana Ave.
Washington, DC 20001
(202) 724-6054

Dade County Advocates for
Victims
1515 N.W. 7th St.
Miami, FL 33125
(305) 547-7933

Victim/Witness Assistance
Project
Metro Atlanta Crime
Commission
100 Edgewood, S.E., Rm. 128
Atlanta, GA 30308
(404) 524-6487

Victim's Kokua Services
4th Floor
1164 Bishop St.
Honolulu, HI 96813
(808) 523-4158

Victim Witness Unit
Ada County Prosecutor's Office
514 W. Jefferson St.
Boise, ID 83702
(208) 383-1237

Victim/Witness Assistance
Program
Rm. 12 D 42
2650 S. California
Chicago, IL 60608
(312) 890-7200

Victim Assistance Program
Indianapolis Police Department
50 N. Alabama
Indianapolis, IN 46204
(317) 236-3331

Victim Services
1915 Hickman
Des Moines, IA 50314
(515) 286-3832

Victim/Witness Program
Attorney General's Office
Judicial Center
Topeka, KS 66612
(913) 296-3315

Victim Information Program
Commonwealth Attorney's
Office
514 W. Liberty St.
Louisville, KY 40202
(502) 588-2300

Victim/Witness Assistance
Bureau
Office of District Attorney
619 S. White St.
New Orleans, LA 70119
(504) 822-2414

Victim/Witness Advocacy
Kennebec County Courthouse
95 State St.
Augusta, ME 04430
(207) 623-1156

Victim/Witness Unit
Baltimore State's Attorney
Rm. 410, Courthouse West
Baltimore, MD 21201
(301) 396-1897

Victim/Witness Assistance
District Attorney's Office
Municipal Court
273 Pamberton Square
Boston, MA 02108
(617) 725-8727

Victim/Witness Program
1441 St. Antoine
Detroit, MI 48226
(313) 224-6645

Victim/Witness Assistance
Program
501 Courthouse
Duluth, MN 55802
(218) 726-2323

Victim Witness Program
Attorney General's Office
P.O. Box 220
Jackson, MS 39205
(601) 359-3680

Victim/Witness Unit
Circuit Attorney's Office
1320 Market St.
St. Louis, MO 83103
(314) 622-4373

Crime Victims Unit
Box 4759
Helena, MT 59601
(406) 444-6535

Victim/Witness Assistance Unit
Lincoln Police Department
233 S. 10th St.
Lincoln, NE 68508
(402) 471-7181

Victim/Witness Assistance
Center
District Attorney's Office
300 S. Fourth St.
Las Vegas, NV 89101
(702) 386-4779

Victim/Witness Service
Hillsborough County Attorney
300 Chestnut St.
Manchester, NH 03101
(603) 627-5605

Victim/Witness Coordinator
Camden County Prosecutors
Office
Parkade Building
Camden, NJ 08101
(609) 757-8462

Victim/Witness Assistance
Program
Prosecutor's Office
Essex County Courts
Building
Newark, NJ 07102
(201) 961-8457

Victim/Witness Center
District Attorney's Office
415 Tijeras, N.W.
Albuquerque, NM 87102
(505) 841-7093

Victim/Witness Service
Project
320 Old Country Rd.
Garden City, NY 11580
(516) 535-3500

Victim Services Agency
3rd Floor
2 Lafayette St.
New York, NY 10007
(212) 577-7700

Victim Assistance Program
825 E. Fourth St.
Charlotte, NC 28202
(704) 336-2190

Victim Witness Program
State's Attorney's Office
P.O. Box 1246
Williston, ND 58801
(701) 572-6373

Victim/Witness Service Center
Justice Center
1st Floor
1215 W. Third St.
Cleveland, OH 44113
(216) 443-7345

Victim/Witness Program
Attorney General's Office
State Capitol Building
Oklahoma City, OK 73105
(405) 521-3921

Victim/Witness Assistance
Program
Rm. 804
1021 S.W. 4th
Portland, OR 97204
(503) 248-3222

Victim/Witness Assistance Unit
District Attorney's Office
2300 Center Square West
Philadelphia, PA 19102
(215) 275-6199

Center for Victims of Violent
Crimes
1520 Penn Ave.
Pittsburgh, PA 15222
(412) 392-8582

Victim/Witness Assistance Unit
Attorney General's Office
72 Pine St.
Providence, RI 02903
(401) 274-4400

Victim/Witness Assistance Unit
District Attorney's Office
P.O. Box 58
Charleston, SC 29402
(803) 723-6714

Victim/Witness Assistance
Program
Minnehana County Courthouse
415 N. Dakota Avenue
Sioux Falls, SD 57102
(605) 335-4226

Victim/Witness Services
303 Metro Courthouse
Nashville, TN 37201
(615) 259-5899

Victim/Witness Program
District Attorney's Office
500 Commerce St.
Dallas, TX 75202
(214) 749-8511

Harris County Victim/Witness
Program
District Attorney's Office
201 Fannin, Rm. 200
Houston, TX 77002
(713) 221-6655

Victim Counseling Unit
Salt Lake County Attorney's
Office
231 E. 400 South
Salt Lake City, UT 84111
(801) 363-7900

Victim/Witness Assistance
Program
Commonwealth Attorney's Office
520 King St., Suite 301
Alexandria, VA 22314
(703) 838-4155

Victim/Witness Services
Commonwealth Attorney's Office
800 E. Marshall St.
Richmond, VA 23219
(804) 790-8045

Victim/Witness Program
341 South Cove Rd.
Burlington, VT 05401
(802) 862-3638

Victim/Witness Assistance Unit
King County Prosecutor
516 Third Ave.
Seattle, WA 98104
(206) 583-4441

Victim/Witness Assistance
Program
Monongalia County Courthouse
Morgantown, WV 26505
(304) 291-7254

Victim/Witness Services
412 Safety Building
821 W. State St.
Milwaukee, WI 53233
(414) 278-4659

The Victim/Witness Program
Rm. 300, The Courthouse
200 N. Center
Casper, WY 82601
(307) 235-9335

·2·

Third-Party Litigation Against the Government

Suppose you hear a noise in another part of your home while you're alone. You call the police with your suspicion that someone has broken into your home. However, the police dispatcher records your address incorrectly, and then gives the wrong address to a police car in your neighborhood. Finding nothing wrong at the wrong address, the police car reports to the dispatcher there is no crime being committed. In the meantime, the person who has broken into your home assaults you and steals your property. If you can prove that the negligence of the dispatcher caused your loss and injury—"proximate cause" is the legal term for this—you may be able to successfully sue the police on the theory that police negligence caused you to become a crime victim.

This is third-party litigation: although you were assaulted and lost property because of a crime committed by someone else, you can sue the police—the third party—because of their negligence.

Selecting a Lawyer

All court cases in this country are based on the adversary system, in which the facts of the case are presented by lawyers for each side to an impartial fact finder, either a judge or a jury. Then the fact finder decides which side will win. The adversary system, however, assumes equal adversaries, something rarely achieved, because the real adversaries in the courtroom are the lawyers for the plaintiff and the defendant. In theory the adversary system favors the party with the best case, but in practice the system favors the party with the best lawyer. Therefore, a crime victim who wants to sue must select a good lawyer. While the victim could represent himself or herself, that is almost certainly going to result in a lost case. No matter how well-educated and intelligent the victim, he or she will be no match for an even moderately talented lawyer.

There are many theories on the best way to select a good trial lawyer. For instance, some people suggest asking your family lawyer (if you have one) or an acquaintance who is a lawyer to represent you. However, your family lawyer, the one who wrote your will or handled your house closing, may not be qualified to represent you in court. Because this lawyer realizes that he or she is unqualified but wants to keep the case, or—more seriously—because the lawyer is unaware that he or she is unqualified, the lawyer may not refer you to an experienced litigator. Ideally, if your family lawyer is unqualified, he or she should say so; that ideal is not always achieved.

As with medicine, the practice of law has become highly specialized. While at one time a lawyer could serve a client's needs in many diverse areas, such as estate planning, real estate, taxes, and business law, the specialized nature of substantive law and procedural rules has made it almost impossible for a lawyer to be a generalist—a person qualified to advise a client in all areas of the law. Litigation is a specialty. For certain types of litigation, a generalist may be sufficient, but third-party litigation requires a knowledgeable and experienced litigator.

How then is the victim to find the litigation specialist? First, a word about how not to do it. Don't look in the Yellow Pages. Letting your "fingers do the walking" may be an effective way to select a plumber, a butcher, or a roofer, but it is not an appropriate way to select a lawyer. Although legal advertising has been permitted since 1977, and although you should not reject a lawyer just because he or she advertises, there are attributes and qualities of a lawyer—particularly a litigator—which you cannot measure by reading an advertisement.

As with most professions, board certification is important although not essential. Some states have board certification for trial lawyers, that is, the lawyer has passed an examination prepared and graded by lawyers that tests the lawyer's knowledge and skill in litigation. The Association of Trial Lawyers of America (ATLA) and other organizations conduct a national board certification program for criminal law and civil law trial specialists. (In fairness, the reader should know that the author of this book is one of the ATLA Board Certification examiners.) If a lawyer is board certified as a trial specialist, a client can be reasonably sure that the lawyer is qualified to represent him or her in court.

However, don't reject a lawyer solely because he or she is not board certified. Your state may not have a certification program, or the lawyer recommended to you may have had neither the time nor the inclination to take a certification examination. Many excellent specialists are not board certified, and it is not unusual for either a younger lawyer or a busy older lawyer to practice without board certification.

What other factors are important? Board certification is a form of peer review, but peer review can be expressed in other ways. If your attorney or a lawyer friend recommends someone as a litigation specialist, that's a recommendation well worth considering.

Most important of all, you should meet and interview the lawyer recommended. Never agree to have someone represent you without personally meeting him or her. After all you may have to spend a great deal of time with the lawyer and may find yourself discussing personal and sensitive matters. Do not employ a lawyer with whom you feel uncomfortable.

Another reason you should interview your lawyer is to find out what the fee will be. Lawyers charge for their services in one of four ways: an hourly rate, a set fee for the legal work to be performed, a contingency fee whereby the lawyer takes a percentage of the judgment (if any), or a combination of an hourly rate and a contingency fee in which the lawyer is paid a specific amount for a certain number of hours, and thereafter has a contingency fee. It is essential that you and your lawyer have a clear understanding of the fees and the method of payment.

In cases in which the client is the plaintiff—the person who files the lawsuit and seeks damages from the defendant—many lawyers charge a contingency fee. If the client wins, the lawyer and the client share the judgment. In many jurisdictions, it is customary for the lawyer to have a one-third contingency, receiving one-third of any judgment. In some jurisdictions the contingency can be as high as 50 percent. However, in contingency fee cases lawyers usually require that the client pay all costs of the litigation, which can include filing fees, expert witness fees, transportation, copying, postage, and deposition costs. The latter refers to the procedure whereby a witness is questioned before trial and a transcript is made of the witness's statement.

In many communities there is a legal aid office. Sometimes that office will represent a plaintiff in a civil case, but more frequently the legal aid lawyers represent defendants in criminal or civil cases who cannot afford to hire a lawyer. In many legal aid offices the lawyers are not allowed to file a case that may result in an award unless two or more private lawyers have turned down the case. Check with your legal aid office if you want to file a third-party case, but you will probably have to be turned down by some private practitioners before you will be eligible for legal aid.

Selecting a good lawyer is an important first step in every third-party litigation case, one that may determine whether you win or lose. It is well worth taking time to consider the available choices.

The Government's Failure to Protect You

In some states, you cannot sue the government even when the negligence of government employees caused you to become the victim of a crime. The reason for this is based on legal history. Many of our laws and rules of procedure come to us from England and that country's common law (judge-made) tradition. One such English law was that the king or queen—the sovereign—could not be sued except under very special circumstances. To some extent, we have continued that tradition in this country, substituting the government for the king and queen. In accordance with these so-called sovereign immunity laws, the government cannot be sued unless it gives you permission to do so. Most states and the federal government have given such permission for certain types of lawsuits; however, civil suits against the government are usually subject to certain limitations and special procedural rules.

For instance, you cannot recover punitive damages—damages greater than your actual losses and which are intended to punish the defendant—against the government on the theory that it is against public policy to force all the people, who are the government, to pay one person's punishment damages. The government is also frequently given greater time to file an answer to a civil complaint because of the widely accepted and probably accurate belief that it will take the government lawyer a longer time to find the responsible individuals within the government to assist in answering the complaint.

However, most states have waived sovereign immunity to permit persons to bring civil actions against the state. In some of these states, the legislature has limited the amount of damages the state can be forced to pay. This limit can be either a dollar amount, i.e., regardless of the amount of the damages, judgment against the state may not exceed $25,000, or a percentage of the damages suffered, i.e., regardless of the amount of the damages, judgment against the state may not exceed 25 percent of the damages.

In most states, the government is not liable for the nonfeasance—failure to act—of police officers in the performance of their duties, but may be liable for the malfeasance—acting improperly—of police officers. Where the police owe a special duty to a particular individual (rather than to society as a whole), however, failure to act—nonfeasance—on the part of the police may result in a successful civil suit against the government. Civil liability on the part of individual police officers, as distinguished from the government, is described on page 35.

Two cases decided by the same court illustrate the special duty rule. In the first, a police informer was murdered shortly after requesting police protection—protection that was not provided. A New York court held that the police have a special duty to protect people who have voluntarily come forward to assist in the arrest or prosecution of criminals once it appears that the informants are in danger due to their cooperation. In a case decided ten years later, the same court held that no such special duty exists when the police are asked for protection by a person who thinks he or she may become the victim of an assault. In that case, the person did become an assault victim, but the court found that the police did not have to provide special protection to everyone who requests it. If you are the victim of or a witness to a crime and cooperate with the police, there may be a special duty on the part of the police to protect you. But the police do not have to protect everyone who requests special protection.

Courts routinely find that the police owe a duty to society as a whole, to all of the people, but not to any single individual unless there is some special relationship. Coupled with sovereign immunity rules that restrict all civil suits against the government, it is difficult for the victim of a crime to sue the government when the police have failed to act to protect the individual.

On a number of occasions, courts have been asked to change the rules that make it difficult to sue the police for failure to protect. Although that might sound reasonable, and although victims have a much better chance of successfully suing the police following some recent court decisions, any wholesale change making the government financially responsible for losses due to crime would almost certainly bankrupt the government. As one court summarized, "We will not impose upon government the obligation to guarantee and assure the health, wealth and happiness of every living person. The law must encourage and protect those subjective values, goals and ideas where possible but it cannot guarantee them. Only human ingenuity, initiative, dignity, love, understanding, and compassion can approach such absolute achievement."

There are many examples of courts denying crime victims recovery for the property losses or the physical injuries they suffered because the police failed to protect the victim and no special relationship or circumstance existed. For example, the Arizona Supreme Court upheld the dismissal of a complaint against a local county that was based on a police officer's failure to stop and arrest an intoxicated motorist before he caused a head-on collision with another automobile which killed three innocent people. A Florida appellate court reached the same conclusion in another head-on crash involving a drunk motorist.

A New York court, however, has recently held that police indifference in the face of an obvious threat may form the basis for a suit by a crime victim. In that case, involving a divorced couple, the family court imposed a protective order forbidding the man from assaulting his former wife and their six-year-old child. This was the fourth protective order issued against him. In one of those decisions that gives the administration of justice a bad name, the court also ordered the father to be given visitation rights. On the first weekend of visitation, the mother brought the six-year-old to her father, who shouted death threats at both her and the child. The mother reported the death threats to police officers who knew of the father's violent history. When the father did not return his daughter at the end of the visitation period, the mother showed the police a copy of the protective order only to be told "just to wait." One police officer urged his superior to send a police car to the father's home, but the suggestion was rejected. During this time the father attacked his daughter with a fork, a knife and a screwdriver, stabbing her in the chest and the back, and then attempted to saw off one of her legs. At the time of trial, the child was permanently disabled both physically and mentally. The father was convicted of attempted murder and imprisoned.

On appeal by the city, the New York Court of Appeals

upheld a $2 million verdict for the child, holding that a special relationship existed between the city police and the child. The court relied on four facts: the existence of the protective order, which was shown to the police; the fact that the police knew of the father's violent history; the police department's response to the mother on the day of the assault, which conveyed the impression that aid of some type would be provided; and the totality of the police conduct in the case.

Although this case is a particularly strong one for the plaintiff, other recent cases suggest that it is getting easier to recover for damages, such as loss of property caused by negligent failure of the police to prevent a crime.

If there is no special relationship, there may be other methods available to establish the liability of local government for the actions (or inactions) of police personnel. For instance, under a provision of the United States Code, if a person is deprived of a constitutional right either as the result of a local government's official policies, or as the result of the local government's failure to train personnel, he or she may be able to collect damages in a civil suit against that government. If police personnel having been inadequately trained results in your becoming the victim of a crime, under the provision of the code, you may be able to sue the government. However, it is not clear that remaining "free" from being the victim of a crime is a constitutional right. If it is not—at least one legal scholar has argued that it should be a constitutional right—then this type of lawsuit would be unsuccessful. While it has been established that persons who are arrested by the police can sue the police, it has not been established that crime victims have the same right.

Witnesses are also entitled to police protection where the police have some notice about the danger. Thus in a case in which the police have arrested a person known to have a violent temper, and have requested someone identify this arrested person, the police owe a special duty of protection to the witness. An Illinois court found that once the police had placed the witness in a perilous position, they had a duty to try to make sure the witness was not assaulted by the person he identified.

Sometimes a special relationship claim leads courts to find distinctions where perhaps there are none. For instance, a New York court found a special relationship between the police and a victim who was shot by her husband when she had a court order of protection but was denied protection by the police. However, one year later, the same appellate court held that no such special relationship existed when the victim repeatedly asked for police protection because her former boyfriend had threatened her, and after police protection was not given she was viciously assaulted by her former boyfriend. The distinction between these two cases—the presence of a court order of protection—is almost nonexistent, for at the time New York law did not permit the issuance of an order of protection unless the parties were married. (For more information on protective orders, see Chapter 5.)

Some courts are particularly reluctant to find a special relationship between police and domestic violence victims even where the police are aware of a danger to the victims. For instance, the California Supreme Court held that a city was not responsible for the death of a woman who asked for police protection—but did not receive it—from her husband who she said was coming to kill her, and who in fact did. The court failed to support a claim for police negligence despite the police having responded to the victim's complaints about her husband twenty times in the preceding year. But in some states, victims of domestic violence have received more protection: a recently enacted statute in Oregon specifically holds police liable under some circumstances for the failure to protect one spouse from another.

In some cases, the victim's own actions may create a special relationship. For instance, one court held that the estate of a homicide victim could sue the government because the victim had been threatened and assaulted for three and one-half years before she fled to government offices seeking sanctuary only to be murdered. Although the decision in this case was based on a number of factors, the court was particularly influenced by the failure of the police to protect the victim in government offices.

However, the failure of the police to act even where potential danger to the victim is known does not always create a special relationship. Thus a New Jersey court found no special relationship between the police and an assault victim where the police, having been notified of a person near police headquarters threatening people with a gun, still failed to investigate the matter.

Police Negligence

In the cases described above, the harm to the victim was caused by the failure of the police to act in some specific way. But what happens if the police do act but act negligently, and the victim is injured by someone else because of this negligence? Although the general principles of sovereign immunity still apply, a lawsuit based on negligent action by the police has more chance of success than one claiming inaction.

For instance, in a widely reported case, a victim called the police emergency number (911) to report a burglary, but the police dispatcher incorrectly recorded the address. When the police discovered the recorded address did not exist, they treated the matter as a crank call and never investigated further. Meanwhile the victim was stabbed to death by the burglar. The court ruled that it was up to the jury to decide whether the recording of the correct address would have resulted in the police arriving in time to prevent the murder. In short, if you call the police, and they do not respond because of an incorrectly recorded address or due to some other negligence, you may have a good case against the police. At the very least, you should discuss this matter with a lawyer.

In another case, the administrator of an estate agreed to cooperate with police who were investigating outbreaks of vandalism. Following the investigation, the estate was vandalized, apparently because of the administrator's cooperation. The estate sued, not because of a special relationship between it and the police, but because of police negligence in failing to recognize there was a potential for retaliation. The court permitted the lawsuit on the grounds that it was up to the jury to determine whether the police had been negligent.

The police also can be negligent when they fail to act despite the possibility of danger to a known victim. Recently, the Arizona Supreme Court found such negligence. An anonymous caller telephoned a local police department to report that an individual's life was in danger. The caller did not reveal either the source of her information or the identity of the perpetrator. However, she gave the name of the victim and said he was in the state hospital and would be released the following day at 4:30 P.M. to spend a weekend at a house in the city in which the call was made. The police dispatcher did not call the state hospital; if he had, he would have discovered that the information provided by the anonymous caller was correct. The dispatcher never warned the victim, and two days later the victim was stabbed twenty-five times and died.

The court found that a reasonable jury might believe the police department had breached the standard of care owed to the victim particularly when there was no attempt to notify him. Again, if you become a crime victim because of police carelessness or inattention, you should discuss the matter with a lawyer.

Many states have abolished sovereign immunity and now permit suits against the government because of the negligent conduct of a government employee. However, even in these states the usual elements of a negligence case must be established, i.e., a duty owed to the victim, a breach of that duty, and injury proximately caused by the breach. Thus a victim in a state that has abolished sovereign immunity would still have to establish some kind of special relationship with the police in order to show that the police officer owed a duty to him or her and not just to society as a whole.

The Federal Government and Sovereign Immunity

Federal government liability for injuries caused to crime victims is described in detail below, but it must be noted here that the United States government has permitted itself to be sued in certain cases. Almost without exception, such cases must be brought in federal court.

The Federal Tort Claims Act does not permit lawsuits against the government when the actions or inactions complained of are discretionary in nature. Thus if a federal official can, but does not have to, undertake a course of action, the act does not permit a lawsuit against the government for the failure of that official to refuse to perform this discretionary, not mandatory, act. The claimant must show that the federal official whose conduct is challenged was acting within the scope of his or her official duties, and not illegally or beyond the scope of these duties.

For example, a woman was recently raped in a United States Post Office lobby after regular business hours but when the lobby was open. The victim sued the government for failure to protect her and prevent the crime from occurring. Evidence showed that on previous occasions, crimes had been committed in and around the lobby and the building. The court ruled that if the government intended to keep the lobby open after regular business hours, it was responsible for providing some security in the lobby; once the postal officials decided to keep the lobby open, it was mandatory—not discretionary—for them to provide this security.

Following the riots which occurred in Washington, D.C., after the assassination of Dr. Martin Luther King, Jr., the government was sued by store owners who suffered property losses during the riots. The claimants argued that the federal government had a duty to protect property in the nation's capital and had failed to do so; however, the court ruled that the decision to use government forces to protect the capital city is a discretionary one not subject to suit under the Federal Tort Claims Act. Generally, this case follows others which have held that the failure on the part of the federal government to provide protection is descretionary.

Personal Liability of Police Officers

The cases described above involve lawsuits against a government agency by the victim of a crime. Typically in such cases the victim also sues the police officer or other government official whom they claim was negligent. Police officers do not ordinarily enjoy sovereign immunity and can be sued individually. In some states, however, statutes have been passed which provide that a public employee is not liable for failure to provide police protection, prevent crimes, or arrest criminals. Also the victim who sues the police officer personally must show that the officer had a special duty to protect the victim, not just society as a whole.

The overwhelming majority of lawsuits by crime victims against the police involve cases in which the officers failed to make an arrest. However, the courts more often than not have found that the officer's failure to arrest the suspect did not involve the breach of any duty owed to the victim. For example, the Indiana Supreme Court ruled that police officers were not liable to the mother of a young girl who was raped and murdered shortly after the police had failed to investigate an earlier rape committed by the same perpetrator. The complaint charged that had the police done their job properly, the criminal would have been arrested, and the subsequent rape and murder would never have occurred. But the court found that even if the police had been negligent, the duty owed was to the general public, not to the rape victim, and thus an essential element of the negligence action was missing.

A Michigan court ruled that a victim wounded by a gun fired during a fight involving many people could not sue police officers who were sitting nearby in their police cruiser, making no attempt to stop the fight. The court found the breach of any duty the police may have committed was a duty owed to the general public, not a particular victim.

Thus although the courts recognize that a police officer may be liable to a crime victim who is injured as a result of the officer's negligence, it is very difficult—some commentators have said it is almost impossible—for a victim to establish that the officer breached the duty owed to the individual victim, as distinguished from the duty owed to the public at large.

The Government's Responsibility for Wrongful Release

Many people become victims of crime at the hands of people who are on some form of conditional release from prison, jail, or a mental hospital. Such conditional release programs include probation, in which a convicted criminal remains out of prison as long as good behavior is maintained; parole, in which a person is released before his or her sentence is completed; and furlough, a limited release from a prison or a hospital at the end of which he or she must return to the facility. In addition, convicted criminals occasionally escape or are wrongfully released through administrative error and may commit crimes that lead to injury and loss to victims.

Richard Thomas was released on parole after serving five years of a prison term. He had originally been sentenced to one to twenty years with a recommendation that he not be paroled. Thomas was diagnosed as mentally disturbed and was a convicted sex offender. The parole officials were aware of an evaluation that predicted he would almost certainly commit a sex-related felony if released. Nevertheless, they did release him and shortly thereafter he murdered a fifteen-year-old girl.

In another case, two women were assaulted by a mental patient shortly after he was released from a hospital. They sued the state of New York, alleging their assailant should not have been released. Research disclosed that the assailant, whose condition was described as "somewhat unusual" by a hospital psychiatrist, had been ordered released a month and a half before the release actually occurred and during this period had several episodes in which he became very violent and had to be physically restrained. However, no reconsideration was given to the release decision, and less than forty-eight hours after the release, the mental patient attacked the two women. The victims recovered a money judgment against the state.

In an Arizona case, Mitchell Blazak was paroled after serving one-third of his sentence for armed robbery and attempted murder. He had a long history of violent, criminal behavior. A psychiatrist found Blazak's case to be "unusual," and described him as a person who should not be released "until some major psychological changes take place . . . [because] . . . he has a definite potential for violence." Shortly after his release, Blazak committed an armed robbery and murdered a victim.

Frequently, psychiatrists play an important role in determining whether a person should be released from prison or from confinement in a mental hospital. While predicting whether someone is likely to commit crimes of violence is, at best, an imperfect science, some cases involve inexcusable amounts of negligence. For instance, some years ago a former high school basketball star kidnapped and sexually assaulted a young girl. He was apprehended and given a twenty-year prison sentence. Thereafter, the judge modified the sentence by ordering him to be placed in the locked ward of a psychiatric hospital, not to be released without permission of the court. However, the psychiatrists at the hospital concluded that their prisoner was no longer dangerous to himself or others—at least not to the extent he had to remain in confinement—and released him on an outpatient status without permission of the court. Almost immediately after his release, the young man went to the very same school from which he had kidnapped his first victim, and kidnapped and murdered another young girl. The victim's parents sued the doctors and settled out of court.

In all of these cases the victims or their representatives sued for wrongful release. In some cases, the victims were successful and in others not. In some cases, the courts ruled a person who has custody of another who is likely to cause harm has a duty to control such a person. In others the courts applied a special relationship test, stating that unless the victim could show that the individual who made the release decision owed a special duty to the victim, the victim could not sue the person who made the release decision. In some cases the courts denied the claims of the victims on the grounds that the person who made the release decision was unable to foresee the danger to the ultimate victim.

Foreseeability is a legal doctrine that asks whether a person who commits a negligent act could have or should have recognized that some risk existed. Where foreseeability cannot be established, where the individual could not possibly have been able to foresee the reasonable or likely consequences of his or her conduct, then most civil actions charging negligence fail.

In some states, a statute gives immunity from civil suits to all state officials who make parole or pardon decisions. For instance, California has such a statute, and in the Richard Thomas case noted above, the case of the mentally disturbed parolee who murdered the fifteen-year-old girl, the courts—and ultimately, the United States Supreme Court—held that such a statute was not unconstitutional even though it prevented the victim from recovering. However, even where there is a state statute giving immunity to state officials, some future case may present the opportunity for a victim to bring an action for wrongful release. For instance, in the Thomas case, the Supreme Court issued a short but important disclaimer: "We need not and do not decide that a parole officer could never be deemed to deprive someone of life by action taken in connection with the release of a prisoner on parole." Thus the Supreme Court has suggested that some parole officials may be liable for particularly inept parole decisions.

In those states in which sovereign immunity has not been abolished, some courts have held the state cannot be sued for wrongful release. However, in the New York case noted above in which two women were assaulted by the recently released mental patient, the court held that the state was liable for the injuries the women suffered even though New York has a sovereign immunity statute that precludes suits based on a discretionary act. The court stated that it was imposing liability, not because of the erroneous medical decision to release, which probably could not form the basis of a civil suit because of New York's sovereign immunity law, but because of the failure of the state officials to review their judgment following the several violent episodes that occurred before the actual release.

In other states, courts have limited the scope of the sovereign immunity statute, particularly where the actions of the releasing authority seem inappropriate. For example, in the Arizona case above in which the releasee had a long history of violent behavior and murdered a woman during an armed robbery following his release, the Supreme Court of Arizona ruled that members of the parole board might not have immunity in cases in which they release a very dangerous prisoner. The court said:

> While society may want and need courageous, independent policy decisions among high level government officials, there seems to be no benefit and, indeed, great potential harm in allowing unbridled discretion without fear of being held to account for their actions for every public official who exercises discretion. The more power bureaucrats exercise over our lives the more we need

some sort of ultimate responsibility to be for their outrageous conduct.

Unquestionably, to parole or not to parole is a difficult
decision. Parole boards do have the responsibility to parole
those prisoners who have been rehabilitated or who otherwise demonstrate that they can safely be returned to society. On the other hand, parole boards also have the
responsibility to deny parole to those who appear to be a
danger to society. While it is impossible to predict with
precision how a person will act when paroled, if strong
evidence suggests the parolee may commit crimes of violence, the Arizona Supreme Court and other courts have
held that parole board members may be liable to their victims.

In the case of the Virginia basketball player who returned
to the scene of his first crime to commit a similar but more
serious crime, the court found the decision of the psychiatrists was grossly negligent—a decision made all the worse
because the psychiatrists were in violation of the court order
allowing release only with the court's permission.

Two other legal doctrines restrict cases in which a victim
can sue a government employee who released an individual
who later assaulted the victim. The first is the "discretionary
function" doctrine, which states that an official with discretionary authority may not be sued because of the consequences of that decision. The theory is that a person with
discretionary authority, a person who can but does not have
to make a decision, will never act where there is any possibility of being held personally responsible for the consequences of that decision. This argument was made to the
Arizona Supreme Court, which prompted the court to respond in the language noted above. However, many states
have a limited sovereign immunity statute that exempts

officials who make discretionary decisions. Note that in the New York case of the two women who were assaulted, it was the officials' failure to review the decision that resulted in the state's liability, not the decision to release.

The second legal doctrine that may prevent a successful civil action against a discretionary decision-maker is that such decisions are the same or similar to those made by judges. For instance, judges routinely decide whether a convicted felon should be sentenced to prison or given probation and released. Such decisions by judges are discretionary; therefore, the argument goes, if the members of parole boards can be held liable for release decisions, why shouldn't a judge be held liable for wrong release decisions? Of course, judges enjoy judicial immunity, which is different from sovereign immunity, but similar in that it exempts a judge from civil suit based on a judicial decision. Nonetheless, judges appear to be influenced by the arguments that equate many of their decisions with those of parole board members.

Crime victims should have the right to sue officials who make inappropriate release decisions. In 1979—the last year for which statistics are available—approximately 61 percent of all persons sentenced to prison were repeat offenders, and 46 percent of them would still have been in prison at the time they committed their next crime had they served their entire term. Even more significantly, over 60 percent of all prisoners released on parole in 1979 were returned to prison within three years. It is no wonder, therefore, that many crime victims suffer at the hands of persons who have been released from prison before the end of their term. At the very least, when the decision to release is grossly negligent, the person who becomes a victim as a result of this release should have the right to challenge the decision. Only three courts, however, have held that a victim has such a right.

The Government's Responsibility for Wrongful Escape

Most courts that have considered cases in which victims have sued prisons and jails or the officers who work in them have recognized that such institutions and their employees may be liable for permitting a person to escape who then commits a crime harming the victim. However, some courts have decided such cases in favor of the government institution or employee on the grounds that negligence on their part was too remote from the actual harm to the victim to be held to be the proximate cause of the victim's injury.

For instance, in a Louisiana case, a trustee escaped from a penitentiary, entered the home of a woman who lived nearby and shot her with a gun he had stolen from a prison employee. During the trial, the victim established through testimony that the escapee who shot her had a long history of violent crimes but, nonetheless, had been promoted to trustee. She also established that there had been many escapes from this prison, making the prison officials well aware of the lack of security. And finally she established that the escapee's possession of the gun was not unusual, that many of the prisoners had access to weapons, as well as to narcotics and alcoholic beverages.

The court held that the state was negligent in permitting the prisoner to escape and that this negligence was the proximate cause of the victim's injury. The inadequate security in the prison, together with the fact that the victim lived near the prison, created a risk area around the prison where the victim lived. The court also held that escape is always in the mind of a dangerous criminal and that leaving such a criminal unattended for hours at a time—as is the case with trustees—is negligent.

However, in a California case, the court found that despite the existence of negligence on the part of sheriff's deputies in permitting prisoners to escape, the death of the victim was not a foreseeable risk. In this case, three prisoners conferring with their attorney in a jury room overpowered the attorney, escaped through an unlocked window, and commandeered a car driven by the victim. The victim was killed when his car, driven by one of the escapees, crashed into an oncoming vehicle. The court held that although the deputy sheriffs might have been negligent in permitting the prisoners to escape, the negligent operation of a motor vehicle by one of the escapees was not foreseeable, and thus the death of the victim also was not foreseeable.

In a West Virginia case, two prisoners escaped from jail, stole a parked car, and while being pursued by a state trooper the next day, collided with another car and seriously injured the occupants. Evidence disclosed that the prisoners escaped as a result of the sheriff giving the jail keys to another prisoner. The court held that the sheriff had been negligent in entrusting the keys to a prisoner, but that this negligence was not the proximate cause of the injury to the victims, nor was it foreseeable that there would be an automobile accident the day after the escape. The court found that the jail officials will be liable for injuries to innocent third parties only when the victim's injuries are the natural and probable consequence of negligence on the part of the officials.

If you become the victim of a crime committed by an escaped prisoner, a lack of foreseeability and proximate cause are two barriers to your successfully suing jail and prison officials. Of course, sovereign immunity laws in your state present another barrier. However, where a prisoner has escaped—or through administrative error is released—negligence has almost certainly occurred. If a victim is harmed in an area close to the place of escape or wrongful release, or if the victim is harmed soon after the escape, there is a greater chance of a finding of proximate cause. Finally, if there have been other escapes from the facility or other administrative errors leading to wrongful release, the courts will usually find that the government officials responsible for security knew or should have known of the conditions that led to the escape, and should have foreseen the risks associated with such lack of security.

When a prisoner is dangerous and has been identified as a risk to society, other legal principles may apply. As a matter of law, a person who negligently creates a risk of harm to someone else is liable for such harm if there is a connection between the negligence and the harm. In the case of a dangerous prisoner who escapes from custody or is released negligently, you as a crime victim may have a cause of action against those responsible for the escape or release, especially if the person was previously identified as being dangerous.

The Government's Responsibility to Warn Victims When Releasing a Dangerous Offender

There are few issues that create as much concern and outrage among victims and their advocates as cases in which dangerous, convicted criminals are released without warning to their potential victims. There have been hundreds, perhaps thousands, of instances of victims being killed or injured by assailants who were known to be dangerous and had prior to their release threatened the very people they injured.

A typical example is found in a 1980 California Supreme Court case. James F., a juvenile offender whose full name was omitted in the court opinion as is typical in cases involving juvenile offenders, had been confined to a local county detention center pursuant to a court order. While confined, James F. was diagnosed as possessing "latent, extremely dangerous and violent propensities regarding young children and that sexual assaults upon young children and violence connected therewith were a likely result of releasing him into the community." The diagnosis further revealed that James F. had stated that he would, if released, "take the life of a young child residing in the neighborhood."

Despite this prediction, the county authorities released James F. to the custody of his mother without warning the local police or the neighboring families of young children. Unfortunately, predictions about James F.'s conduct were accurate: within twenty-four hours of his release, he murdered a five-year-old boy in the neighborhood.

The victim's parents sued the county officials for wrongful release and for failing to warn the parents of young children in the neighborhood where James F.'s mother lived. The court ruled that the decision to release was a discretionary one, and, pursuant to California's sovereign immunity statute, discretionary decisions were immune from challenge. The court then turned to what it described as the "most troublesome contentions" of the parents of the murdered child, "namely, that (the) County is liable for its failure to warn the local police and the parents of neighborhood children" that James F. was being released. In deciding this issue, the court referred to the threat in question as a "generalized threat to a segment of the population." It contrasted this case with an earlier one in which a youthful offender with "homicidal tendencies and a background of violence and cruelty" had been released to foster parents without informing them or other members of their family of this background. The foster mother was attacked, sued the state, and was permitted to maintain her action on the ground the state owed a special duty of care to her because the release of the offender created a foreseeable peril. In the case of the five-year-old murder victim, however, the court ruled that the county owed no special duty of care to the victim because there was no foreseeable peril. The court said:

> Bearing in mind the ever-present danger of parole violations, we nonetheless conclude that public entities and employees have no affirmative duty to warn of the release of an inmate with a violent history who has made nonspecific threats of harm directed at nonspecific victims.

It is sad to note too that the court described the rationale for its decision as one based on risk versus benefit, and the cost of the benefit, often referred to as risk/benefit analysis. First, the court reported that hundreds of thousands of people are released every year on some form of probation or parole and are under the supervision of a small number of public officials. To require the warning of potential victims of the releases, the court said, would force the state to hire more officials to give the warnings, increasing the cost of the system.

Second, the court said, warnings would stigmatize the releases, and there would be relatively little benefit to society because many threats do not create a real peril. In fact, the court found that, "notification to the public at large of the release of each offender who has a history of violence and who has made a generalized threat at some time during incarceration or while under supervision would, in our view, produce a cacaphony of warnings that by reason of their sheer volume would add little to the effective protection of the public." Stated somewhat differently, so many warnings would be given that people would begin to doubt their validity.

Unfortunately, the opinion of this court is typical of cases that allege a failure to warn potential crime victims. In a

1976 case, a psychotherapist was told by a patient that he intended to kill a young woman he knew. The psychotherapist asked state university police to detain the patient and the police did, but then released him when he appeared to be rational. The police, who knew the name of the threatened young woman, failed to warn either her or her family. Shortly thereafter, the patient killed the young woman. The court ruled that there was no special duty owed by the police to warn the victim, and in the absence of such duty, the police could not be sued because of their failure to do so.

In another case, a man was released on bail following his arrest for assault and resisting arrest despite assaulting a police officer and damaging property while in jail. The man was known to have a violent temper. He was released on bail, nonetheless, and within three hours killed a young man. The family of the victim sued the jail authorities, but once again the court found the releasing authorities owed no specific duty to warn the victim.

Courts have found public officials at fault for failing to warn the victim of a crime that a certain danger existed in cases where an official had promised the victim or local officials that a warning would be given if the offender was released. For instance, a sheriff and his deputies were sued by the survivors of a murder victim who was killed by a man released on bail. Earlier, the victim had made a complaint against the offender, who was then arrested and the sheriff and his deputies promised to warn the victim of any impending release of the defendant. However, when the defendant was released, nobody warned the victim. The court ruled that an unfulfilled promise to warn that results in the victim being hurt or killed is actionable and constitutes negligence on the part of the officials who promised to warn the victim.

A $1 million verdict was returned for the wrongful death

of a thirty-one-year-old woman and her eight-year-old daughter murdered by a prisoner on work release. The woman had been raped by Charles Campbell and she, along with one of her neighbors, had testified against him at his trial. He was convicted of sodomy and assault and sentenced to up to ten years in prison. The State Board of Prison Terms and Paroles waived his minimum 7½-year term, allowing Campbell to be placed on work release. In retaliation for her testimony against him, Campbell went to the thirty-one-year-old woman's home while on work release and murdered her, her daughter, and the neighbor. The mother of the murdered woman brought suit against the state and various officials of the department of corrections, the parole review board, and the prison. She alleged that the parole officials' decision to waive the minimum term and allow work release was negligent because it was not based on accurate information: the board did not receive records of infractions that Campbell committed in prison. The state admitted liability.

Several federal courts have found Veterans' Administration Hospital staff officials negligent for failing to warn local law enforcement officials of the impending release of a patient who had been referred to the hospital by the local officials based on the patient's violent behavior. Where the person released assaulted someone, the victim could sue the government. Again, the unfulfilled promise constituted negligence.

Without a specific threat against you or specific promise to warn you, public officials appear to have no duty to alert you of the release of a prisoner, even where the risk is obvious and imminent. The courts have held it is unrealistic and too expensive to impose such a duty on those who have the authority to release offenders with a history of violent behavior.

Government Liability for Failure to Protect Students

In most states, a public or private school is liable for negligence when it fails to exercise care in protecting students, care in this context meaning the conduct a reasonable and prudent person would use to prevent crime.

Students usually become victims of crime from one of four sources: strangers who invade school grounds or students, teachers, or strangers who attack the child off campus. Schools are generally not liable for attacks that occur off campus unless the student was young and the school was negligent in allowing him or her to leave the school grounds. These are essentially lack of supervision cases. Although some courts have held that it is negligent for school personnel to permit a child to leave the school grounds, other courts require the plaintiff to show it was foreseeable the child would become the victim of a crime before school personnel may be held liable for permitting the child to leave. In addition, in some states, school personnel are immune from such lawsuits according to applicable sovereign immunity statutes.

In a recent case in Arizona, a ten-year-old girl volunteered to take home a neighbor's dog that had wandered into the school. She took the dog to the principal's office, where permission to take the dog home was denied. Somehow, nobody was sure how, she left with the dog, was abducted within a few blocks of the school, and was killed in a nearby field. The Arizona Supreme Court held that school personnel could not have foreseen that the child would leave the school grounds, nor could they have foreseen that the child would be harmed. Therefore, the parents' lawsuit against the school was dismissed.

However, a California court ruled that the parents of a coed who had been raped and murdered in a state university dormitory could sue the state on the grounds the university was negligent in failing to provide security in the dormitory. Similarly, a New York court ruled that a student could sue a state university following her assault in the basement of a dormitory. In this case, there was evidence that university personnel had failed to lock the doors of the dormitory despite frequent complaints that strangers had entered the building.

Universities and colleges seem to have greater responsibilities toward their students than schools do toward younger students, partly because universities and colleges act as landlord as well as educator. As noted in the next chapter, a landlord—whether as university or in a more traditional form—has a duty to protect tenants from becoming victims of certain types of criminal activity.

Despite the increase in the number of child victims, schools continue to enjoy immunity when they are sued by the parents of victimized children. Many courts seem willing to accept the fact that a school cannot protect each and every child except within the confines of the school. If a child leaves the school, therefore, unless the school has been negligent in permitting the child to leave, the school is not at fault if the child becomes the victim of a crime.

When a child is assaulted by a teacher, a successful lawsuit against a school may be possible if the child's parents can show: that the school was negligent in hiring the teacher, that such negligence was the proximate cause of the assault, and that the school failed to supervise the teacher. When a child is assaulted by another student, the parents must show the school was negligent in preventing the assault by failing to provide the supervision ordinarily provided by schools, and that would have prevented the assault.

With assaults by teachers, most courts are reluctant to find a school at fault unless the teacher has a history of such behavior, and the school was or should have been aware of such behavior. In addition, corporal punishment by teachers is permitted in some states. Where it is not permitted, the courts nonetheless recognize that a teacher is entitled to maintain order in a classroom, and that at least some touching of students may be required to do so.

With assaults by fellow students, courts are generally very reluctant to hold the school at fault unless the school is aware or should have been aware that a particular student is likely to assault another.

The Changing Trend

Legal principles are worth noting, but if you are the victim of a crime and you reasonably believe the government is at least partially responsible, what would you do? Some of the cases described in this chapter do not favor the crime victim, some do. How do you determine whether your case is a good one?

Obviously, the first thing is to discuss the matter with a lawyer. You also may wish to keep in mind that there appears to be an increased willingness on the part of many courts to find that government officials were negligent. Legal trends are difficult to measure—particularly in this country of over seven thousand courts—but it appears that crime victims are receiving more sympathetic treatment when they file suit against the government or a government employee.

For instance, during 1985, a Connecticut federal court let a verdict stand of $2,600,000 awarded to a crime victim who alleged that the police virtually ignored her calls for help. She had complained to them for eight months that her husband was threatening her life. A court order of protection prohibited the husband from being with his wife. When he came to the house, the victim called the police, who took twenty-five minutes to respond, during which time the husband coaxed her out of the house and stabbed and punched her. When the police finally arrived, they watched the husband kick his wife several more times before restraining him.

At the trial the police argued that they were reluctant to interfere in domestic arguments in order to promote domestic harmony. The court held, however, that the victim had made it clear by repeatedly calling for help that she did not want to resolve the dispute in a domestic setting.

Obviously, the decision in this case rejects the view that the police have no special duty to protect. Other recent cases also seem to reject this view, but whether there is a trend in this direction remains to be seen.

Recently, two federal appellate courts held that it is negligent for government officials to withhold information from the parole board about an eligible parolee's potential danger to the community. These courts stated that while the decision to parole may be discretionary, an official may not withhold information that would help the parole board members make the correct decision.

Other recent cases support the rights of crime victims to sue the government when government negligence was at least partially responsible for the harm they suffered. In short, every crime victim who believes government negligence is responsible for the crime occurring should try to learn whether he or she has a worthwhile lawsuit.

·3·

Third-Party Litigation Against Private Individuals and Institutions

Third-party litigation against private parties is more common than such litigation against government agencies or employees. As noted in the preceding chapter, litigation against the government involves special substantive law and procedural rules that tend to protect and favor the government. But third-party litigation against private parties is similar to other litigation and is generally not subject to special rules.

Suppose you rent an apartment and, because your landlord wants to save money, he fails to fix the broken lock on the front door of the building so that nothing prevents strangers from entering. Someone unlawfully enters the building and assaults you in the elevator. Assault is a crime as well as a civil wrong, and if you can identify your assailant, you can sue him even if he is not prosecuted. Of course, your assailant may not have any money, making any such suit futile. But what about the landlord? If his failure to fix the lock directly led to the assault—"proximate cause" is the legal term for this—you may be able to sue him on the theory that his negligence caused the injury to you.

The Liability of Landlords for Crimes Committed by Third Parties Against Tenants

Until very recently, landlords have been under little or no duty to protect tenants from criminal attacks by third parties. A number of reasons are given for this lack of landlord responsibility, including the policy of requiring the police—and not private persons—to protect people from criminal acts. In addition, a landlord's failure to provide security may have little or nothing to do with the fact that a tenant became the victim of a crime.

Recently, however, some courts have begun to decide otherwise. One of the first cases to hold a landlord responsible occurred in 1970 when a federal court found that the landlord of a large apartment complex was in the best position to know what dangers existed. The court noted that the landlord knew more about crime prevention in the apartment complex than either the police or the tenants. The written lease between the landlord and the tenant also required the landlord to keep in effect certain security arrangements that existed when the plaintiff signed the lease. However, by the time the tenant became the victim of an assault in the apartment hallway, these security arrangements had been changed. The court compared the landlord/tenant relationship with the innkeeper/guest relationship which has always required the innkeeper to provide reasonable protection to the guest from criminal acts committed by third parties.

Although other courts have reached similar decisions, it is important to note the law does not require a landlord to guarantee the physical safety of a tenant. For instance, in the above case, the court found that the landlord not only had reduced the amount of the security in the apartment complex, but also knew there had been many assaults and robberies in the complex, particularly after security had been reduced. Under those circumstances, the court said, the landlord's negligence in failing to maintain the security that existed when the tenant signed the lease created the necessary connection between the negligence of the landlord and the assault on the tenant.

A few courts have refused to hold landlords liable for crimes committed against tenants on the theory that their relationship does not create a duty for the landlord to protect the tenant. Other courts have held that a landlord who does not reduce the amount of security after the tenant signs the lease is not liable to the tenant if this security is not sufficient.

However, to the extent there is a trend, an increasing number of landlords are being held responsible for the criminal acts committed by third parties against tenants. Some courts base the liability on the landlord's obligation to maintain hallways, elevators, lobbies, stairwells, and other so-called common areas—areas used by all tenants—in a reasonably safe condition. Others have found liability where the landlord was aware that numerous crimes were being committed in the apartment house but did little or nothing to increase security.

Landlords have been held liable in cases in which they failed to provide adequate lighting in common areas, failed to provide locks on doors leading to and from the outside of the building, failed to install security locks on the doors of apartments, and provided insufficient lighting in the apartment complex or building parking lots.

In still other cases, landlords have been found liable to tenants because of the landlord's affirmative conduct. In one case a landlord was held liable to a tenant raped by a man to whom the landlord had mistakenly given the tenant's key. In another instance, a landlord was held liable for hiring a janitor who sexually assaulted a number of tenants. If the landlord had investigated the janitor's background the landlord would have discovered he had been convicted of raping a tenant and kidnapping her son while employed in another building. Sadly, that is one of a growing number of cases of landlords hiring convicted felons without bothering to verify references or credentials, and then having the employee commit a criminal act against a tenant.

In 1975, the Michigan Supreme Court advanced the rights of crime victims by holding that under some circumstances a landlord has the duty to investigate the risks of crime, even where there have been no criminal acts reported. In that case, a Michigan state clinic leased space in the landlord's building. A mental patient being treated by the clinic assaulted the employee of another tenant. Tenants had complained to the landlord about the mental patients visiting the building. The court held that even in the absence of any reported assaults, the landlord had a duty to investigate whether increased security arrangements were called for in light of the presence of mental patients in the building. Of course, this Michigan case also concerned the rights of tenants in commercially leased space as distinguished from a residence. Such tenants are also entitled to at least some landlord concern for security.

A few courts have extended the doctrine of "implied warranty of habitability" to cases in which tenants have been the crime victims. Implied warranty of habitability is a legal principle stating that in addition to the written or oral terms of a lease, the landlord warrants—guarantees —that the premises are such that a person can live in them. If a tenant discovers that an apartment has no heat, or is infested with insects, or has a ceiling that leaks, he or she may be able to move out before the end of the lease on the ground that it is impossible to live in the apartment. A few courts have held that the implied warranty of habitability includes the implied (not written) warranty that the apartment is safe and if that is not true, the tenant who becomes a crime victim may sue the landlord for the failure to provide adequate security.

Sometimes, regardless of the circumstances, courts are unwilling to extend landlord liability to the protection of tenants who become the victims of crime. A Pennsylvania trial court held that a $6 million verdict against a landlord, $3 million of which were punitive damages, was justified under the circumstances of the case. An intermediate appellate court upheld the verdict, but reduced the amount of the award. Three men attacked a husband and wife as they parked their car in an indoor parking lot adjacent to their apartment building. The assailants robbed the couple at gunpoint and kidnapped them, taking them to another location where the woman was sexually assaulted by all three assailants.

In their lawsuit against the landlord, the victims showed that there had been many crimes committed in the parking lot against other tenants. They also showed that a private security service had suggested to the landlord a number of security improvements, none of which was adopted. The parking lot was poorly lit, and the entrances were not controlled. The trial court held that a landlord who acts or fails to act in complete disregard of a high risk of harm to a tenant may be liable for punitive damages.

On appeal, the landlord convinced the intermediate appellate court that the punitive damage award to the husband should be reduced by one-half. However, the Pennsylvania Supreme Court set aside the entire award to the victims and ordered a new trial, stating that a landlord's duty to protect tenants concerns only injuries caused by the landlord's negligence in maintaining the premises. In such cases, the landlord is liable for injuries resulting from a condition of which the landlord knew or should have known; the landlord's duty could not be extended to criminal acts committed by third persons. The court compared the duty of a landlord to protect tenants to the duty of the police to protect society as a whole; police are not liable for failing to protect specific individuals, and a landlord is similarly not liable for failing to protect particular tenants. On retrial, the Supreme Court ordered the trial court to charge the jury that a landlord has no general duty to protect tenants against criminal acts by third persons unless the landlord has specifically agreed to do so. The Supreme Court ruled that the punitive damages issue could not be considered by the jury if the only evidence the plaintiffs presented showed that the security systems were inadequate. Punitive damages could only be awarded if the plaintiffs proved that the landlord's conduct was malicious, wanton, reckless and willful. Negligence, even gross negligence, does not establish willfulness, the court stated.

The California Supreme Court has reached the opposite conclusion. In this case, the victim was an anesthesiologist employed at a hospital who was shot in the chest during a robbery attempt in the hospital's parking lot. He sued the hospital, claiming it was negligent in failing to provide adequate security measures for the parking lot. The trial court granted the hospital's motion to dismiss because the doctor was unable to prove the hospital had notice of prior crimes of the same or similar nature, and thus was unable to establish foreseeability on the part of the hospital.

The California Supreme Court reversed this decision, holding that evidence of prior similar acts is not necessary to impose a duty on property owners to anticipate and to protect against possible criminal acts by third persons. The court found the idea of a landowner not being bound to anticipate criminal acts if such acts haven't already occurred to be fatally flawed because, first, it discourages landowners from taking adequate measures to protect premises they know are dangerous until and in fact someone is injured, and second, it leads to some silly distinctions, i.e., how similar must the acts be, how close in time, how near in location, and so on. The court also noted the arbitrary nature of a similar acts rule: the first victim loses and all subsequent victims can recover.

Both Florida and Texas courts have reached a similar result. The Florida court also recognized that the Florida Residential and Landlord-Tenant Act imposes obligations upon the landlord, requiring, among other things, locks and the safe condition of common areas.

In another case, there was evidence the landlord had agreed to provide security. A jury awarded a rape victim $500,000 after she was sexually assaulted inside her apartment. The landlord had advertised the apartment as being in a building that had "security" and a "security system." However, the four-hundred-unit complex employed one security guard who patrolled from 10 P.M. to 6 A.M., and who also was employed almost one hundred hours per week in another job. There were no exterior locks on the building. The trial court ruled that the victim had a right to rely on the landlord's advertisement that the building had a security system and therefore had been misled. Evidence in this case disclosed over one hundred crimes against tenants in the apartment building in the two years immediately preceding the rape of the victim.

Occasionally, the terms of a lease permit a tenant/crime victim to sue a landlord. An Illinois jury returned a verdict of $175,000 in favor of a woman who had been kidnapped from her apartment and raped. She had leased an apartment from a landlord who had advertised that a burglar alarm system came with each apartment. The tenant's lease required the landlord to repair broken appliances on the premises with due diligence and after her burglar alarm became inoperable, she made repeated requests that it be repaired. Seven months later, with the burglar alarm still broken she returned home one day and was accosted by an armed man waiting inside her apartment, who forced her into the trunk of her car, drove her to a remote area, and then raped her. Testimony at the trial revealed that if the burglar alarm had been working, the assailant would have activated it when he gained entry to the tenant's apartment. Of the $175,000 verdict, $125,000 was for actual damages, and $50,000 was for punitive damages.

In at least one case the violation of a city ordinance was held to be evidence of a property owner's responsibility for a third person's criminal act. In this case, a ten-year-old girl was taken from a sidewalk outside the apartment where she lived and dragged across the street to a vacant and dilapidated apartment in the defendant's apartment complex. There the girl was sexually assaulted. There was evidence of prior similar acts having been committed in the defendant's apartment complex during the two previous years.

The trial court in this case found that a Dallas, Texas, ordinance that established minimum standards for owners, and which admittedly had been violated in this case, was not applicable since the victim—who had been kidnapped—was not on the property with the defendant's knowledge or consent. Thus she was a trespasser, admittedly an involuntary one, and the defendant's only duty to her was to refrain from injuring her through acts of gross negligence.

The Texas Supreme Court reversed the decision. The Supreme Court held that the victim was a beneficiary of the ordinance in question, being a member of the group or class the legislature sought to protect, and that the harm suffered by the victim was the type of harm the legislature sought to minimize or prevent when it passed the ordinance. Because many cities have ordinances requiring owners of abandoned buildings to have them sealed, demolished or continuously guarded, this recent decision may prove to be useful in other cases.

The way in which an apartment is advertised, the terms of the written lease, the existing security measures in the apartment or commercial building, and the amount of crime in the building are some of the important issues that courts look at in determining whether a landlord can be liable when a tenant becomes the victim of a crime.

The Liability of Hotels and Motels for Assaults Committed Against Guests

In November 1974, Connie Francis, a well-known singer, was sexually assaulted at knifepoint in a Howard Johnson Hotel by an assailant who entered her room. At the trial, Ms. Francis established that her assailant had gained entry through an unlocked, sliding glass door.

She sued Howard Johnson for failure to provide her with a safe room, showing at the trial that the door through which her assailant had entered could be opened simply by moving the door back and forth. Other evidence showed that in the preceding ten months, rooms in that hotel had been burglarized four times by people entering in the same manner as Ms. Francis's assailant. The hotel countered with evidence that more secure locks for the patio doors had been ordered months before but had been delayed by a United Parcel Service strike.

Ms. Francis's alleged damages included lost earnings, expenses for psychiatric care, and diminished quality of sexual relations with her husband. The jury awarded her

$2.5 million and, while pending on appeal, the case was settled for $1.5 million.

This case received a great deal of national attention, but it was also one of the first of a growing number of cases in which hotel and motel owners have been sued by victims of crime for failing to take reasonable measures to protect them.

Verdicts in favor of such victims have become almost routine. For instance, a Milwaukee, Wisconsin, jury awarded an elderly man over $600,000 following his being attacked and beaten in a hotel where he lived as a permanent guest. The evidence included testimony by former hotel security guards that they had requested the management to increase the security staff because they feared for their own safety, but management denied the request. A Tallahassee, Florida, jury awarded $220,000 to a hotel employee who was beaten and robbed as she prepared to leave the hotel. Evidence showed there had been sixty-six crimes committed in this hotel during the eighteen months before the assault on the employee. A Washington, D.C., jury awarded two women over half a million dollars after they were raped in a downtown motel that had a sign in the lobby claiming a closed-circuit television system provided security to the premises. Unfortunately, at the time of the assault, there was only one television camera, which was pointed at the cash register for the purpose of protecting motel property. The motel also was in a high-crime area.

Another Florida jury, this one in Orlando, awarded a sexual assault and robbery victim $1.25 million in her action against a Howard Johnson motel (half a million of that amount was for punitive damages and was set aside on appeal). In the six-month period before the assault, there had been thirty reported crimes on the premises, some of which involved assaults on guests.

In contrast to the law concerning a landlord's liability,

hotel operators have always been liable—at least to some extent—for injuries to guests caused by third parties. While the law has never required a hotel operator to ensure the safety of guests, the law has always required hotels to exercise at least some care in protecting their customers. This has been particularly true where the hotel owner knew there was some danger to the guests. In recent years the risk to guests appears to have increased because of the construction of large motel and hotel complexes in relatively isolated and remote areas of large cities, and as urban renewal increases, some hotels have been constructed in high-crime areas.

A review of over one hundred cases of crime victims successfully suing hotel or motel operators or settling out of court reveals several types of lawsuits caused by a number of different security problems. From the review it seems more appropriate to classify these cases by the type of hotel negligence leading to the crime than by injury to the victim.

Security Personnel

While no state or municipality requires a hotel to maintain security personnel on the premises, some courts have permitted crime victims to claim that it was negligence, under the circumstances, for the hotel to fail to employ security personnel, and that if guards had been present, the assault would not have occurred. Frequently, expert testimony is required to establish how many security personnel would have been needed to prevent the crime.

In the Orlando, Florida, case described above, the victim presented expert testimony establishing that three full-time guards would have prevented most criminal acts, including the attack on her, as well as the thirty reported crimes that had occurred on the premises in the previous six months.

An Illinois court instructed a jury that it could consider

whether or not security personnel would have prevented an intruder from reaching the upper floors of a hotel where he assaulted a guest.

Another Illinois jury was asked to consider whether existing security personnel were numerous enough to protect the guests, considering the known danger. The hotel in question had over two thousand rooms on twenty-three floors, and in the six months preceding the particularly vicious assault described below, there had been numerous cases of people being attacked in their rooms. The hotel employed a security force of five on each shift, with three given stationary positions, while the others patrolled the twenty-three floors and the lobby floor. Two women shared a room in the hotel while attending a conference. One woman left the room for a few minutes and upon her return was attacked by a man who had already assaulted her roommate. One of the women was murdered, and the other was seriously injured when the assailant tried to cut her throat.

Testimony at the trial revealed that the former chief of security at the hotel had recommended to the management that additional personnel were necessary to provide adequate security. The hotel owners, however, did not follow the recommendation. Four times as many security officers per shift were required to make sure that minimal protection for the guests was available. The trial court had directed a verdict in favor of the hotel, but an appellate court reversed the decision, holding that there should be a trial in which the victims could demonstrate that the hotel had been negligent in failing to increase its security force.

Even fewer security personnel were present in a 1,200-room hotel in which a husband and wife were attacked by an armed intruder. On the night of the incident, the hotel had one security officer on the premises, one room clerk, and one bellboy, despite most of the hotel rooms being occupied, and a dance being in progress with hundreds of guests. A state statute exempted a hotel owner from liability if the owner exercised reasonable care to protect guests, but the court ruled the jury could consider whether, under the circumstances, the hotel's negligence was so serious as to constitute a lack of reasonable care.

Lack of Proper Response by Security Personnel

Even assuming adequate security, some victims claim that hotel security personnel respond inappropriately after an attack.

In the case of the hotel with 1,200 rooms described above, after the couple reported the assault, many minutes passed before the hotel security guard came to their room. A similar claim was made in the Connie Francis case where an additional claim was made that the responding security personnel questioned Ms. Francis in such a way as to make her think they believed she had invited the man into her room or had made up the whole story as a publicity gag— all in the face of her obvious physical injuries.

Even more bizarre was the case of a Texas woman who was attacked by a man as she came out of her motel room. He forced her back into the room, tied her up, and sexually assaulted her. He threatened to murder her and said he would return. She managed to call the front desk, and told the desk clerk who she was, reporting she was still bound. She gave her room number, told the clerk she had been sexually assaulted and robbed, and that her assailant had threatened to return. After a long period of time of talking to a number of different hotel personnel, she was finally told that the police had been called and that nobody from the hotel would come to assist her until they arrived. She was then told to hang up the telephone, apparently because she was tying up the hotel switchboard. When the police finally arrived, they found that several hotel managers had been waiting outside the victim's room for nearly a half hour, ignoring her screams for help.

At trial the hotel argued it had fulfilled its duty to the guest by calling the police. The trial and appellate courts rejected this argument, described the hotel employee's conduct as callous, and affirmed a $78,000 judgment against the hotel.

Closely allied to this issue of inadequate or inappropriate response are the cases in which hotel employees detect suspicious persons on the premises but fail to order them to leave. In a number of cases, courts have ruled that the mere presence of an intruder on an upper floor of a hotel constitutes evidence the hotel was negligent in detecting and evicting intruders. In still other cases, courts have said it is negligence for a hotel security officer to observe a stranger on the premises but not investigate to determine whether the person is a guest or an intruder. Hotels are particularly subject to judicial criticism when there have been reports of criminal activity in the hotel, and hotel personnel still fail to investigate if a stranger is legally on the premises.

Closed-Circuit Television as a Security Requirement

Those cases in which the hotel's failure to install television monitors forms the basis of a negligence claim generally rely on one of a number of issues. First, some hotels, and many motels, because of their architectural design—long hallways, numerous stairways and elevators, common rooms, and parking lots, many at a considerable distance from the front desk—require television monitors as a crime deterrent. Large hotels or motels that sprawl over an acre or more present difficult security problems, some of which can only be addressed by the installation of television monitors.

Second, where a hotel or motel advertises that it uses

closed-circuit television monitors to protect guests, the claim must be accurate, and the equipment must be operable. In addition, there are reported cases of hotels with operable closed-circuit televisions that had nobody assigned to watch them to report what the cameras observed.

Finally, where television cameras are used, they must be placed to give the best possible field of vision in the most appropriate locations. In the Washington, D.C., case noted above, the one television camera on the premises was placed to protect the hotel, not the guests. That is not a legally sufficient use of closed-circuit television to prevent or reduce a hotel owner's liability for injury to a guest.

Hotel Liability Because of Room Key Mistakes and Negligence

Of course, an intruder does not have to lurk outside a hotel room, or force open a room door, if he or she has the room key. If an intruder can gain entry by merely jiggling the door, as in the Connie Francis case, breaking down the door is unnecessary. Courts have upheld awards to victims when evidence showed that an intruder had been handed the key to the victim's room by the desk clerk in the mistaken belief that the intruder was traveling with the victim. In other cases, intruders have acquired room pass keys from hotel maids or other personnel. Intruders have also duplicated pass keys, or have gotten keys from a locksmith that would open almost any door.

Although state statutes do not require hotel and motel owners to use a particular type of lock, some cases have been decided on the basis of the type of door lock. For instance, one court permitted a victim to introduce evidence at trial showing that most hotel room doors have chain locks and peep holes, while the hotel in which she was assaulted had neither. In another case, a victim showed that the type of lock on the room door that an intruder had successfully picked was the lowest quality lock that could be purchased, one not accepted by most hotel operators.

In many cases in which victims claim an intruder gained entry through a locked door, the hotel or motel owner argues that the door in question was equipped with a chain lock that the victim failed to use. Although the law here is not the same in every state, the majority of courts will permit a jury to consider whether a victim was negligent as well by failing to use the chain lock. If the court finds the victim's own negligence led to the commission of the crime, it may reduce the victim's award or dismiss it altogether.

The Liability of Hotels and Motels for Theft of Guest Property

Essentially, hotel and motel patrons lose property in one of three ways: thefts by hotel or motel employees, thefts by intruders when guests are not in their rooms, and thefts committed as part of another crime, such as an assault. Regardless of how the crime is committed, some—but not all—of the same issues described in the preceding section apply. To determine whether a hotel owner is liable for the loss of a victim's jewelry, for example, the kind of security on the premises is an important issue.

However, many states have enacted laws that limit a hotel or motel owner's liability for the loss of a guest's property regardless of whether the owner was negligent. These laws provide that a hotel owner must have a safe or other secure place in which a guest may keep valuables and must notify each guest—usually by posting a sign in the room—that the hotel has such a place where the guest may keep valuables. Finally, most statutes require the sign to contain information concerning the limits on the owner's liability if the guest fails to place the valuables in the safe.

As a result, many courts have held a hotel owner's liability is reduced or eliminated (depending on the applicable statute) if the guest did not place valuables in the hotel safe, which were then stolen. A few courts have held that a guest does not have to give all valuables to the hotel for safekeeping, particularly where the valuables consist of relatively small amounts of money or inexpensive jewelry. Where such items are stolen, the guest's failure to place the items in the hotel safe is not a bar to the victim suing the hotel. Finally, some courts have ruled that notwithstanding a state statute limiting a hotel owner's liability for lost or stolen property not placed in a safe, where the hotel has been grossly negligent—as distinguished from simple negligence—such a statute does not prevent the theft victim from suing the hotel.

A California court held that a hotel was liable for the loss of a guest's money when it purchased a safe, posted a notice that it was not responsible for lost or stolen property, but failed to state on the notice that the hotel owned a safe.

In a recent Louisiana case, a young desk clerk mistakenly gave the room key to an intruder who then robbed the occupants at gunpoint. Because of their occupation, the robbery victims traveled with large sums of money, which they elected not to place in the hotel safe, losing over $25,000. There was evidence, too, showing that the one hotel security guard on duty was sound asleep when the robbery occurred.

Despite a state statute exempting hotel owners from any liability for property stolen by force or as the result of not being placed in the hotel safe, the state supreme court held the statute was not applicable in this case because of the gross negligence of the hotel staff.

In cases in which guests deposit valuables in a hotel safe, the courts impose the standard of an insurer on the hotel if the guests' property is stolen. This standard essentially holds the hotel owners to a very strict standard of care and diligence to protect the property given to them for safe-keeping.

The Liability of Other Business Establishments and People for Crimes Committed by Third Persons

Hotel owners and landlords are only two of the business proprietors who can be sued by crime victims because of the criminal acts of another. Essentially, no business proprietor is immune from third-party litigation, although in the case of some business institutions it is extremely difficult for a victim to establish negligence on the part of the third party. However, crime victims have established third-party liability on the part of many different business concerns.

In the cases described in this section the victim may not have been the target of the criminal's conduct. In the following instances the plaintiff—the victim—usually was not the target of the crime; someone else or a business entity was the target. Thus the legal principle involved concerns the extent to which a third party has a duty to protect a person legally on the premises of the business when a crime occurs, the result of which is the victim being injured.

Banks

It is extremely difficult for a victim injured in a bank robbery to sue the bank successfully for third-party liability. The law is clear: a bank must maintain the bank premises in a reasonably safe condition. However, just because a bank is frequently the target of armed robberies does not mean the bank must use extraordinary care to protect customers, nor does the fact that a bank safeguards its depositors' money create any special duty of care whereby the bank ensures the physical safety of the depositors. In addition, a bank customer is an invitee, a legal term that means only ordinary care is required to protect the customer. Finally, although bank employees are required to react swiftly during a robbery, the courts do not require the employees to act with the same prudence that would be required if the employees had time to think about their choices. In other words, when faced with an emergency, a person does not have to act with the same degree of care as the person who acts after reflection.

In one of the very few cases in which a court allowed a bank customer to sue the bank, the court noted that the bank was in a position to warn the customer of the danger but did not. A teller at a Pennsylvania bank was handed a note by a robber which stated he was carrying fifty sticks of dynamite, which he would detonate if not given money. The teller handed the note to a bank officer who went to another bank in the same building and returned with two of that bank's security officers. Meanwhile, a customer entered the bank to cash a check and was approached by a bank officer who knew a robbery was in progress and knew of the bomb. The officer invited the customer to have his check cashed at a window near the robber, not warning the customer of the robbery or the bomb. When the security officers tried to arrest the robber, he detonated the bomb, killing himself and one security officer and injuring a number of people, including the customer who was cashing his check.

Under the circumstances of that case, the Supreme Court of Pennsylvania stated it was up to the jury to determine whether the bank was negligent in failing to warn the injured customer of the robbery in progress in which the robber was holding—or at least claimed to be holding—a bomb.

Where banks use floor-to-ceiling bulletproof glass, it is

not uncommon for bank robbers, who cannot gain access to the tellers' money drawers, to threaten to kill a customer if the teller does not permit access through a locked door. However, if that threat is made, and the tellers refuse to follow the robber's instructions, and a customer is murdered by the robber in retaliation, the courts have held the bank is not liable for the death of the customer. The courts have determined that banks do not have to accede to criminal demands, and that any rule requiring them to do so might be against public policy because it would encourage bank robberies through hostage taking.

In summary, banks have practically no legal obligation to protect customers from crimes committed by criminal intruders.

Storekeepers

Like banks, storekeepers have a general duty to exercise ordinary care to protect customers from injuries caused by criminal acts. However, because one individual is rarely under a duty to protect another from a criminal attack by a third person, a storekeeper is not under a duty to protect customers from crimes that could not be foreseen or anticipated. Storekeepers do not ensure the safety of their customers, and if they act reasonably during a robbery, it is very difficult for someone injured during the course of the robbery to bring an action against the store. While a storekeeper may be negligent if he fails to warn customers of a known danger, the courts are divided on whether there is a duty to warn a customer in a situation where the store has been the object of numerous robberies, and the police have hidden in the store in the hope of capturing felons during additional robberies.

For instance, a California court held that a store which had been robbed twice by the same individual, and had police hiding in it, with the store security personnel expecting a third robbery, was not negligent in failing to warn a customer who was injured when the anticipated third robbery occurred. The opposite conclusion was reached by a Georgia court in a case in which a store security officer shot a patron while trying to prevent a robbery.

The right of the storekeeper to use self-defense is described in Chapter 8. This right is neither greater nor less than the general duty of care—the legal requirement that the condition of the premises and the conduct of the storekeeper not be injurious to a patron—the storekeeper owes to the customer. Thus when a customer is injured by a storekeeper or employee using self-defense to prevent a robbery or assault, the cases are decided on the basis of whether the amount of force used was reasonable under the circumstances, and whether it was foreseeable that this force would cause injury to innocent third persons. A storekeeper can use self-defense to protect store property, but the selection of the force must be reasonable, taking into account the danger to customers.

Of course, if a storekeeper is aware that a robbery may occur—on the basis of frequent past robberies or a specific threat of one—and fails to take any precautions at all, the storekeeper may be liable to victims injured during a robbery. While there may be no duty to warn customers of an anticipated robbery (even when the police have staked out the premises), there is a duty to use reasonable security personnel or devices to prevent robberies.

The duty to prevent robberies is based on foreseeability. For instance, an Oregon court held that even when a store is located in a so-called high-crime area, the owner is under no duty to have security personnel, alarms, or special lighting to discourage criminals. On the other hand, if the store owner was told a robbery would occur at a specific time, there might be a duty to install special devices or procedures to protect customers at the designated time.

Like bank officials, storekeepers do not have to comply with the demands of a person committing a crime. If a customer is injured because the storekeeper does not comply with these demands, it is very unlikely the customer will be able to sue the owner.

If a customer voluntarily tries to stop the robbery or voluntarily comes to the aid of a storekeeper, there is no third-party liability on the part of the storekeeper for any injury suffered by the customer. That was essentially the situation in a Louisiana case in which a customer was shot and killed after deciding to fight with the robber.

Shopping malls present some unique issues. While the liability of storekeepers in a mall is the same as any other storekeeper, shopping malls have common areas between stores and almost inevitably have large parking lots. There is some duty for the malls to provide security in the common areas, particularly if there are substantial distances between store entrances. Some courts have compared this duty to the duty owed by a landlord to tenants to provide safe conditions in the common areas of an apartment house.

It is in the parking lots, however, where shopping malls have had the greatest exposure as third-party defendants. A North Carolina court ruled that when thirty-six criminal acts had been reported in the parking lot of a large suburban shopping mall in the year preceding the assault on a customer in the lot, it was up to the jury to determine whether it was foreseeable the victim would be assaulted and whether the shopping mall owners were negligent in failing to provide greater security.

If a shopping mall parking lot has lighting and is routinely patrolled, the victim of a criminal act may have difficulty establishing negligence on the part of the mall owners. Like shopkeepers, the mall owners do not ensure the safety of patrons in all parts of the mall, nor can the owners anticipate all criminal acts.

Theaters and Coliseums

Theaters and coliseums also present special problems. Frequently, they are dark and contain hundreds or even thousands of people. Sometimes the entertainment offered seems to attract an unusual number of ill-behaved patrons. Rock concerts may create special hazards in this regard. A review of the case law presents an unusually large number of third-party lawsuits in which victims of crime have been assaulted and/or robbed at rock concerts. Many theaters and coliseums also are adjacent to large parking areas which, like the parking lots of shopping malls, are frequently the place where crimes are committed.

Generally, theaters and coliseums have the same duty toward their patrons as do stores: they have a general duty of care to protect their patrons but are not the ensurers of their safety. However, because of their size and the great number of people on their premises, theaters and coliseums appear to have a somewhat greater duty to have security personnel. Theater and coliseum owners also appear to be held to a higher standard of care than other proprietors if prior criminal acts have occurred.

A survey conducted several years ago showed that in cases in which a victim was assaulted in a coliseum or theater, the victim was unable to prove negligence almost twice as often as he was able to prove negligence. For instance, an Ohio court found that despite there having been a number of robberies and assaults in a coliseum during recent rock concerts, the robbery of a patron during such a concert was not the result of negligence on the part of the coliseum. In this case, twenty security personnel, some in uniform and some in plainclothes, patrolled the facility during the concert. While more security personnel might have prevented the crime from occurring, the court found that twenty personnel was not an unreasonably low number even though the court took into account the greater duty of care this type of facility owner has to provide for security personnel.

However, if the coliseum knew that a particular customer had assaulted others in the past, and failed to evict this customer or offer special protection to others, the coliseum might be negligent for any assault committed by the customer. These were essentially the facts of a Florida case in which a young man was seriously injured by a person known to have a history of assaults. Although the security personnel saw the assailant enter the coliseum, and knew he had a history of picking fights with other patrons, they made no attempt to evict him, nor did they pay particular attention to his actions.

In some cases, theaters and coliseums serve alcoholic beverages, and if they do they may have an additional duty not to serve liquor to people who appear to be intoxicated.

Transportation Companies

A bus, train, or airplane corporation, or any other business that transports people for a fee—referred to in the law as common carriers—have special duties of care that vary according to the state and to whether the customer is in the vehicle or waiting for it at a terminal or platform.

Common carriers have a general duty to protect passengers from criminal acts committed by third persons. When carriers knew or should have known a crime was likely to occur, they are liable if the passenger is assaulted and the carrier did nothing to protect them. In some states, a common carrier is held to a high degree of care to protect passengers but in others the carrier's duty is described as "ordinary care." Even in those states with the high degree of care, the standard applies only to crimes occurring on a vehicle, and not to crimes occurring in a terminal or station.

With assaults in a vehicle, the employee in charge of the vehicle—the driver, pilot, conductor, etc.—is the person examined by the courts to determine whether there was negligence. Such negligence frequently takes one of two forms: either the employee's conduct was responsible for creating the danger to the passenger, or the employee knew or should have known of the danger but did not assist the passenger.

For instance, in Pennsylvania a number of passengers were injured by a group of young men who boarded their trolley and assaulted them; the court found the driver negligent. When the driver stopped his trolley at a corner, the young men began to throw objects at it, but instead of moving the trolley away, the driver chose to wait. Some of the young men entered the trolley and assaulted passengers. By then, the driver was unable to move the trolley and made no attempt to alert the police, sound his horn, or even leave his seat. The court found the driver negligent in failing to move the trolley as soon as it was struck by objects and further negligent in failing to seek help during the assault.

Sometimes the common carrier's employee actually causes the assault on the passenger. In a Georgia case, the driver of a bus became involved in a violent argument with several people waiting to board the bus. One of the people threw an object at the bus that broke a window, seriously injuring the passenger next to it. The court denied the bus company's motion to dismiss, stating that it was up to the jury to determine whether the driver had been negligent. An Illinois court reached a similar conclusion when a bus driver started an argument with the owner of a stalled car blocking the street. The car owner became enraged at the driver and attacked a passenger with a tire iron.

Common carriers can be held liable if a passenger is assaulted while waiting in a terminal or station. However, they do not necessarily owe the same duty to people who are waiting for passengers, or who have entered the station for another reason. In short, the assault victim must have the status of a passenger in order to claim liability.

Frequently in these assaults, there has been a history of criminal acts committed on the premises. For instance, in Illinois a passenger who was waiting for a train was severely beaten by two unidentified men. The train company knew of several robberies that had occurred in the same train station and an adjacent one. There was no patrolman on duty, nor were any other transit personnel present. The court stated that once a common carrier knows of criminal acts on its premises, it must take reasonable steps to make sure passengers are safe. A New York court reached the same conclusion when a woman was sexually assaulted in a remote area of a train station that had no patrolman.

When a common carrier's vehicle arrives at a terminal, the carrier's failure to provide a safe place to disembark can lead to third-party liability. In a Florida case, an interstate bus arrived at 4:15 A.M. at a closed terminal in a high-crime area. While walking away from the terminal, a passenger was assaulted. The court stated that if the terminal will be closed at the end of a trip, the common carrier has the duty to warn the passengers before the trip begins.

The Liability of Employers for Hiring Felons Who Thereafter Commit Crimes

If an employee injures another person—either accidentally or deliberately—the employer may be liable to the third person under the doctrine of "respondent superior," a legal principle holding that the employer may be liable for the injuries caused by the employee. However, for such liability to be established, the employee must be working within the scope of his or her duties. For instance, if a house painter on a lunch break robs a bank, the employer would not be liable to the bank because robbing banks is not within the duties of a house painter. However, if the house painter drops a container of paint that strikes and injures a by-stander, the house painter's employer might be liable for the employee's negligence.

But what about crimes employees commit that are closely connected to their work? For instance, suppose the house painter, after gaining entry to your house to paint some rooms, assaults you? Could the employer be held liable?

The answer to this question depends in part on whether the house painter had a criminal record, and whether the employer knew of it. An employer may be under no duty to determine if an employee has a record, but if the employer knows of such a record, the employer may be held liable for criminal acts committed by the employee, according to many court rulings.

For instance, the Michigan Supreme Court held that while employers do not guarantee that an employee has no crim-inal record, if they know or should have known of such a record, the jury may determine negligence if the employee comes in contact with the public and assaults a person doing business with the employer.

This duty of care in hiring imposed on employers is dif-ferent from the duty arising out of the doctrine of respon-dent superior. Almost by definition, a criminal act committed by an employee will not be part of the employee's duties, making the doctrine of respondent superior inapplicable. But if the crime victim can establish that the employer was negligent in hiring an employee with a criminal record, the employer may be liable for the employee's conduct.

For instance, a Texas trial court upheld a verdict of $5 million in damages against a taxicab company for hiring a criminally violent driver who raped and robbed a passenger in the presence of her two young children. The court held there were two fundamental rules basic to this case: first, common carriers are required to use the utmost caution in protecting passengers, a rule that applies to airlines, railroads, taxicab companies, etc. Second, common carriers and their employees are liable for assaults by the employee under this duty to protect passengers. A number of recent cases have held employers liable for the negligent hiring and retention of a violent-prone employee who injures others in the course of his work.

The negligence in this case was particularly horrendous. The driver had seven previous felony convictions, including another rape and assault charge filed only three months before the cab company hired him. The company conceded at the trial that it had made no independent check or investigation of the driver's background.

If an employer is aware of an employee's criminal record but the record is a minor one, the employer probably will not be found liable for the employee's criminal conduct. For instance, in a District of Columbia case, an employee once convicted of public intoxication was hired to work in an apartment house, and thereafter stole jewelry from a tenant. The court found the employer was not negligent in hiring the employee.

It is sometimes difficult for an employer to determine whether an employee has a criminal record. In some states, an individual can request a "statement of no record" whereby the local law enforcement agency will check its records and, if a person has no criminal record, will state so on a printed form. However, such a statement does not indicate if the individual has a criminal record in another state. Every state also has privacy laws that limit access to criminal records. As noted in Chapter 1, it is frequently a condition of parole or probation for people to be employed. If there were a system that permitted employers to learn whether applicants had criminal records, some applicants would never be hired and would be denied probation or parole.

Finally, some people respond truthfully to the question on an employment application asking if they have a criminal record. If the answer is yes, an employer may have a duty to investigate the nature and extent of the criminal record. Similarly, if an employee is charged with a crime while employed, the employer may have a duty to investigate the charge to determine whether the employee should be discharged even though the employee has not been convicted. Thus one court held that an employer who knew an employee had been convicted of rape and was charged with a second rape while employed had a duty to investigate whether the employee—who frequently came into contact with the public—should be fired.

If an employee is armed, the employer has an even higher duty of care to make sure the employee does not have a criminal record. A Texas court ruled that an employer had negligently hired an armed security guard, who stated on the employment application that he had a criminal record. The employer did not investigate further, or he would have learned the employee had a long criminal record. While on the job the employee shot the employer's customer.

The Duty of a Person to Protect Another from a Criminal Act

Almost without exception, the cases described in the preceding sections describe situations in which the law recognizes a special relationship between the victim of crime and the person who has third-party liability for the crime. But suppose there is no such special relationship: is there a duty to protect another person from a criminal attack?

Except in the very rare instance of someone knowing of an extraordinary criminal danger, no one is under a duty to protect someone else. When an extraordinary danger is known, there may be a duty to warn potential victims, but there is no duty to protect them or to intervene to stop the crime from being committed. Research does not indicate any people without a special relationship to the crime victims being held liable for failing to protect them.

Recently, a number of states have passed hit-and-run statutes that require a driver involved in an accident to stop and help any injured person. In addition, some states have enacted laws that require certain people to report incidents of child abuse. And a few states recently have passed laws requiring a person who sees another in danger to give reasonable assistance.

There are a number of special relationships not described above in which the law imposes a duty on one person to protect another from crime. Some courts have held that an employer must provide a safe place to work; an employee who becomes a crime victim because of work conditions or environment may have reason to sue the employer. This is not always true as there are several rulings in which the courts imposed no liability on a bank for tellers being injured during the course of a robbery. There are cases, however, of employers knowing of existing dangers and failing to protect the employees, and then being held liable for criminal attacks against the employees.

Hospitals may have a duty to warn employees or other patients about particularly dangerous patients.

People who employ babysitters may be liable if the baby-sitter is assaulted by someone or by the children.

The Maryland Court of Appeals has held that a handgun manufacturer may be strictly liable under some circumstances for gunshot injuries caused by the criminal use of one of its handguns. In addition, the court held that if the gun in question is a "Saturday night special" ("a cheap, short-barrelled, lightweight, easily concealable handgun, commonly of shoddy construction"), then strict liability may be imposed upon the manufacturer or anyone else in the marketing chain, including the retailer. Liability is limited, however, to a case in which the plaintiff is killed or wounded by such a weapon. In addition, the shooting must be a criminal act.

Do you have a worthwhile third-party lawsuit against a person or an institution? Obviously, this is a question to be answered by a lawyer. But when trying to decide whether to consult a lawyer, or even whether to get a second opinion if your lawyer advises that you do not have a worthwhile action, ask yourself the following questions: Did some kind of special relationship exist between you and someone else—a landlord, an innkeeper, a storekeeper, etc.? If so, could the person with whom you had such a relationship have prevented the crime? Do you have damages caused by the crime? If so, you may be able to sue a third party and recover all or a portion of your losses.

·4·

Children

The smallest victims may be the most numerous, so numerous, in fact, that it is impossible to count them all, especially since victimization of children is perhaps the most underreported of all crimes.

Some special rules and procedures have evolved during the past few years to assist the child victim, but parents should remember that they too become victims when their child is assaulted or abused. While the criminal justice system in many states has made accommodations for children, no such accommodations exist for their parents, who play an important role in helping the child victim through the intricacies of this system. While the child can look to the parents for help, the parents may also want and need such support, both for their own sake and the child's.

But parents can do more than offer comfort and information to their child victims by guarding against crimes in several ways. First, while they should teach safety at home, schools have such a responsibility as well. Make sure your child's school has a child-safety program that is more than merely having a police officer visit once a year to tell the children to look both ways when crossing the street. A number of sophisticated and well-planned instruction plans over several days will teach children about the dangers of certain types of people, what to do if approached by strangers, how and where to report an unwanted touching, how to use safety devices such as a telephone, when to just plain call for help, and other self-protective actions children should know.

You may also wish to find out whether your state requires the licensing of and security checks for institutions and people who work with children. Sadly, many instances of child abuse have been committed by people working with children who were previously convicted of such crimes. In most states it is more difficult to become a taxi driver or bartender than to become a person put in charge of the custody or safety of children. These taxi drivers and bartenders must establish they have not been convicted of a serious crime, but such a security check is frequently not required for a person to run a day care center.

It may be an invasion of privacy to require teachers and others who routinely work with children to submit to fingerprint checks or other security analyses, but this is a small price to pay for protecting society's smallest and perhaps most vulnerable victims.

If child psychologists are correct that children, particularly young ones, are unlikely to fantasize about sexual abuse, parents should be particularly alert to any such stories. In addition, children eight or older sometimes are able to recount in a straightforward manner incidents which an adult would have great difficulty discussing. Just because a child seems to be very matter-of-fact about reporting a serious crime—even his or her own victimization—does not mean the story is untrue.

If your child tells you a crime has been committed, listen carefully to determine whether the child is describing an actual event. Decide which appropriate authority the crime should be reported to. Depending on the age and maturity of your child, you may want to tell him or her about the responsibilities and duties of the officials the child will see.

The first and perhaps hardest issue facing many parents of child victims is whether to view the criminal justice process with suspicion. Will dealing with police, prosecutors and the courts cause even greater trauma for their child than the crime did? Parents should be aware of the new rights for child victims, described below, designed to lessen the difficulties a child may have as complainant or witness. The choice of letting a child become a complainant—the person who reports a crime—is not an easy one, but the more parents are willing to do so, the fewer child victims there will be.

If your child has been a victim, it is best to have a child psychologist or other expert conduct the first interview, and it should be videotaped. Some police and prosecutors are not specially trained to interview child victims or witnesses and may not know the best way to obtain accurate information. The number of times a child is required to talk about an unpleasant experience should be kept to a minimum, so an accurate first interview is very important.

If your community does not employ specially trained personnel, you be the expert. Explain to the child what is going to happen; introduce the child to the police and prosecutor and explain their roles. If criminal charges are filed and your child is required to testify, take the child to court to show him or her the courtroom, and if possible, let the child meet the judge before the trial. Push for your child's special rights as a victim, with the possibility of videotaped testimony or testimony via closed-circuit television, procedures described below. Where these devices are not used—even where they are—if the child is young enough, ask permission to hold the child on your lap while he or she is testifying.

It is important to note that not all children can testify in court or can testify against a defendant. The general rule in most states is that every person is assumed to be capable of testifying in court unless some question is raised about his or her competence. For children, as one court described it, the question is whether the child is "sufficiently mature to receive correct impressions by his or her senses, to recollect and narrate intelligently and to appreciate the moral duty to tell the truth." Mental capacity and maturity differ between children; some are simply not mature enough to testify, while others clearly have a sound understanding of what the truth is and why it should be told. Several years ago in a case I prosecuted, a six-year-old girl was the only eyewitness to a homicide. As is typical with a child witness, the judge, an elderly and experienced jurist, questioned the child in court, but out of the presence of the jury, to determine whether she was competent to testify. The judge asked her age, and a few questions about school and family. He asked her if she knew that telling the truth was important, and the child responded that she knew that truth telling was indeed important.

"Well," continued the judge, getting to the crucial question, "is it right to tell a lie, or wrong to tell a lie?"

The child looked thoughtful for a moment (while I held my breath), and then with more charm than I believed possible in a six-year-old, she looked the judge square in the eye and replied, "Well, that depends on who you're telling it to, your honor, and that's no lie!" The judge, of course, ruled that the child was competent to testify.

Child Abuse and Neglect Laws

Both the increase in reported crimes against children and the total number of such crimes describe a national tragedy. The American Humane Society reported 413,000 cases of child abuse in 1976 and in 1981, 851,000 cases. By 1983 the number had risen to 953,000. That is one case of *reported* child abuse every thirty-three seconds of every minute of every hour of every day.

After examining a great many surveys of child abuse, one national organization reported that as many as 25 percent of all girls and as many as 10 percent of all boys in the United States are the victims of sexual molestation at least once during their childhood. Reported child abuse cases support at least part of this finding because most victims of sexual molestation are girls, and the most common molester is a male family member.

Finally, the University of New Hampshire Family Violence Research Center reports that between 2 and 5 million American women suffered an incestuous sexual event at least once during childhood.

In short, there are hundreds of thousands of child victims every year—perhaps more—and there are millions of Americans who, as children, were the victims of violent crime.

Child *neglect* is abandonment, refusal to provide needed care or to secure medical assistance, inadequate physical supervision, permitting or encouraging chronic truancy, and inadequate nurturing and affection. Every state has child neglect laws that take the child away when parental neglect can be established.

Child *abuse* is assault with a weapon or physically injuring the child with one's hands, sexual assault, close confinement by tying up a child or locking him or her in a room for a long period of time, and emotionally or physically abusing a child through any means, causing the child to be incapable of functioning as a normal person.

A "child" is anyone not yet eighteen. Although neglect and abuse of infants and very young children may be the most underreported type of abuse for obvious reasons, on the basis of reported cases it appears that older children are more likely to be abused or neglected. Adolescents suffer at more than twice the rate for elementary school children who suffer at almost twice the rate for preschool age children.

There are also dramatic differences between the sexes with respect to abuse and neglect. The physical abuse of males decreases with age, but increases with age for females. Adolescent girls are eight times more likely to experience sexual abuse than adolescent boys.

Every state has a child abuse and neglect law that typically requires certain people to report child abuse or neglect, creates procedures for criminal courts and family courts to resolve accusations of abuse or neglect, and establishes special agencies or departments to investigate such cases.

Like spouse abuse, child abuse and neglect is greatly underreported because the victim frequently depends on the abuser emotionally and economically. Unquestionably, therefore, there is a need for special legislation to require certain people to report suspected incidents of neglect or abuse, with a failure to report leading to criminal prosecution or a civil suit for malpractice. Mandatory reporters usually include teachers, physicians, social workers, or anyone else who, because of their employment or duties, comes in contact with children.

To encourage such reporting, most state statutes also grant both civil and criminal immunity to anyone who does report abuse or neglect. This immunity offers protection in a number of ways. First, assuming good faith on the part of reporters who believe there has been abuse or neglect, reporters are protected from being sued if they are wrong. Second, a reporter cannot be fired, demoted, or disciplined in any way for making the report. Third, reporters who are health care professionals may treat a child for neglect or abuse without the consent of the child's parent and without threat of a lawsuit for malpractice. Different states have different protections for those who report abuse, and it is essential to consult your statute for clarification if you believe you may be required to report child abuse.

Mandatory reporting laws are controversial. By requiring reporting, they may interfere with privacy rights that victim advocates believe are more important than reporting crime. For instance, almost all rape crisis centers permit a sexual assault victim to use the center without first reporting the assault to law enforcement officials. The centers believe the decision of whether or not to report is up to the victim, and almost without exception, local law enforcement authorities respect the centers' view.

But what if the victim of a sexual assault is a child, a situation that requires a report by law? Should the rape crisis counselor be held to a different standard depending on the age of the sexual assault victim? These are hard questions. On the one hand, a sexual assault victim should have rights of confidentiality and not be required to report a sexual assault in order to receive what may be badly needed counseling. And the crisis counselor should not be forced to breach the victim's confidentiality, possibly causing unwanted publicity about the assault.

On the other hand, child victims of abuse may not possess sufficient maturity or judgment to be able to make a decision about reporting their own victimization. At the very least, when a child reports being abused to a counselor, and the abuser is in a position to hurt the child again, the counselor should be required, even at the risk of breaching victim confidentiality, to report the crime to protect the child.

Although there is some authority to the contrary, the general view is that patients and clients of doctors and lawyers, who enjoy a statutory or court-established privilege, lose that privilege if they reveal that they are the victim or perpetrator of child abuse. In short, doctors and lawyers may be required to reveal child abuse when they learn of it. Several years ago, the California Supreme Court held that a doctor who fails to report child abuse can be held liable for subsequent abuse of the child on a theory of medical malpractice.

However, very few people have been prosecuted or sued for not reporting child abuse or neglect, and the courts have not had an occasion to balance the legitimate interests of victim confidentiality and prevention of child abuse.

Suppose the child abuser is a member of the family? What happens to the victim? Every state has procedures to remove a child victim from the home. These procedures seek to balance the parents' rights to be free of governmental interference—and the similar rights of children—with the government's desire to protect children. Almost without exception, states permit the police to take a child victim into protective custody when his or her life or health is in danger. Some states permit health care professionals to refuse to release a child to the custody of parents following treatment when the professional believes the child's life or health is in jeopardy.

Except for emergency situations, most states require a court order to remove a child from the custody of a parent, even if the parent is the abuser. Some states do have emergency procedures that don't require a court order. However, if a court order has not been issued, and the child victim has been removed on an emergency basis, the parent or guardian will be granted a court hearing, usually within three or four days. Of course, a child removed from home goes to a shelter or foster home, which may provide an environment only slightly better than what the child has left.

Limits on Child Abuse

Sometimes there is a very thin line between child punishment and child abuse. A parent or guardian is permitted to discipline a child and may use reasonable physical punishment to do so. Any parent or guardian of children, or any adult who has supervised children for long periods of time, knows that there are times when some punishment is both reasonable and necessary. Under what circumstances, therefore, are you a reasonable parent, and under what circumstances are you assaulting a child? State legislatures and the courts have wrestled with this question for a long time.

To establish that an act was legitimate punishment rather than abuse, first, the person who inflicted the punishment must be a parent, guardian, or someone acting at the request of either. In approximately one-third of the states a teacher may inflict physical punishment on a child without the permission of the parent or guardian.

Second, the physical punishment must have been inflicted as discipline for something the child did that was wrong. Many states describe this as "promoting the welfare of the child," thus not allowing punishment for an act the child omitted rather than committed.

Third, regardless of the severity of the wrong committed by the child, the punishment cannot be allowed to create a risk of death or substantial bodily harm. In almost all states, extreme pain and extreme mental distress and disfigurement are specifically excluded as permissible punishments.

But there are other problems in determining if a child is a victim or has merely been punished.

For instance, as anyone who has spent time with children knows, what causes extreme mental distress to one child may be totally ineffective as punishment for another. Some parents rarely, if ever, inflict any physical punishment on their children, preferring instead to reason with or persuade them toward appropriate behavior. Other parents believe that a swift spanking is the best teacher. It is not always easy to determine when a child has been physically abused and when merely punished—more severely than some might believe is prudent, but still within legal limits.

In trying to balance the interests of the three parties— the child, the parents, and the states—at a hearing to terminate parental rights most courts have adopted some important procedural rules.

First, such cases are tried by a judge, not by a jury. Neither the United States Constitution nor state law requires that there be a jury in this type of case. As with most family issues that end up in court (divorce, adoption, etc.), legal scholars believe judges are better able to decide the factual issues, as well as the legal issues, than juries, which are comprised of nonlawyers. Second, a lawyer is assigned to represent the interests of the child, since almost everyone acknowledges that the child's interests may be different from both the parents' and the state's. Third, the state must establish by "clear and convincing evidence" that the child has been abused or neglected and should be removed from the custody of the parents or guardian. A "clear and convincing" standard means less evidence is needed to convict than in a criminal case ("proof beyond a reasonable doubt"), but more than is needed to win in a civil case ("proof by a preponderance of the evidence").

Some people have suggested that there are no winners in a parental rights termination proceeding; the child loses the companionship of a parent, the parent loses the child, and the state must take on the expense of child rearing. However, where abuse and neglect exist and can be proven by clear and convincing evidence, the child must be a "winner" when removed from an abusive or neglectful relationship.

The Criminal Justice System and Child Abuse Cases

Although there are special rules, procedures, and even special courts for cases involving the termination of parental rights, a parent or other adult who is accused by a child of committing a criminal act is treated like any other defendant. But children are different from other victims, and very slowly the courts and legislatures have altered the procedural rules in order to permit their more humane treatment while at the same time preserving the defendant's rights of due process. One problem associated with child victims is the inability of all children, and particularly very young children, to describe their experiences. And while a court is a strange and frequently hostile environment for many people, it can be particularly so for a child. And children are particularly vulnerable to cross-examination by a defense attorney, whose obligation may be to test the truthfulness and accuracy of the child's testimony.

In a number of ways, child victims are treated differently than adults. For instance, most state courts permit a child who is the victim of a sexual assault to testify through the use of anatomically correct puppets or dolls. Thus children can show the judge or jury what happened, even if they cannot describe the act, or don't know the names for parts of the body. An adult would not be permitted to use such devices.

Pretrial procedures also recognize the child's inability to verbalize experiences. Police officers and prosecutors, who are trained to question victims in a nonleading way, use leading questions when addressing children to establish if a crime has been committed. Children often become confused through repeated questioning, which can lead to inconsistencies even when the child is being both candid and truthful. While inconsistencies in an adult's story might indicate a lack of both candor and honesty, law enforcement personnel know the same is not necessarily true of children.

Police and prosecutors also employ child psychologists and other professionals to assist in investigations, a practice that has been criticized on the grounds that it interferes with the defendant's constitutional rights because the state is providing too much assistance to the victim. Frequently, however, children—and some adults—must be told there is nothing wrong with reporting the acts of an adult, even of a relative or friend. A psychologist will almost certainly have to help child victims explain what happened, leading them through a description in a way that might be inappropriate for an adult victim.

The practice of preparing a child to be a witness presents a confusing anomaly. On the one hand, research indicates most children under the age of seven do not have the capacity to lie. One study analyzed over three hundred sex abuse cases of children seven and younger, concluding that less than 4 percent of the children had lied. On the other hand, studies suggest that jurors rarely, if ever, vote to convict when the only evidence of the crime comes from the testimony of a young child. Although in most states the uncorroborated testimony of a child is sufficient to convict a person of sexual abuse, corroborating evidence is almost always required before a jury will return a guilty verdict.

However, even when the child does testify, some states require the trial judge to caution the jury about the weight to be given to the child's testimony. The jury is told that because the child is not as mature as an adult, they may give less value to this testimony.

If a child does testify, how do the states ensure that the trial will not victimize the child even more than the crime did? More than twenty states permit a child to testify without actually appearing in the courtroom. In some states, two-way, closed-circuit television allows the child to be in a separate room while the people in the courtroom—the jurors, the judge, the lawyers, etc.—can watch on a television screen. The child can see the questioner on a television screen in his or her room where frequently a parent, friend, or child psychologist is present.

In some states, the child's testimony is videotaped before the trial and then shown to the jury. Although in most states where this is done both the prosecution and the defense counsel can ask the child questions, that is not always true. In a few states, a child psychologist or a child services expert asks questions while the prosecutor and the defense counsel watch and sometimes may submit questions to the child services expert. To date, seventeen states have enacted videotaping statutes for the benefit of child victims (Alaska, Arizona, Arkansas, California, Colorado, Florida, Kentucky, Louisiana, Maine, Maryland, Montana, New Mexico, New York, Oklahoma, South Dakota, Texas, and Wisconsin), and eleven states have enacted special hearsay exceptions for the same purpose (Arizona, Colorado, Florida, Illinois, Indiana, Iowa, Kansas, Minnesota, South Dakota, Utah, Vermont, and Washington).

All such procedures are intended to protect the child victim from the pressures and trauma of actually appearing in court. Unfortunately, however, the legitimate interests of the victim do collide with the rights of the defendant. Under the Constitution, a criminal defendant has the right to confront and cross-examine his or her accusers, because of the so-called confrontation clause of the Sixth Amendment. Does testifying by closed-circuit television, or by videotape, or without the defense attorney actually asking the questions, satisfy the confrontation clause? In late 1984, one state appeals court held that it does not. The Supreme Court of the United States will almost certainly have to decide this issue because another appellate court in a different state held that such a procedure does satisfy the confrontation clause.

Another example of courts altering rules to protect the child victim involves the hearsay rule. "Hearsay" is a statement made by a person other than the person testifying. For instance, if you told a police officer that John Smith robbed you, and at Smith's trial the police officer recounted what you had told him, his testimony would be hearsay. Obviously, the statement is being offered in evidence to prove that Smith robbed you. In fact, a police officer cannot testify about what a victim said regarding a crime.

There are many exceptions to the hearsay rule. For instance, the law has always permitted a police officer, or anyone else, to testify about what a crime victim said while dying. The law's view is that people who know they are dying will always tell the truth. There are other traditional exceptions to the hearsay rule—and recently, for child victims, a new exception. Seven states now permit the hearsay statement of a child under the age of ten when the child accuses someone of sexual abuse, and the trial judge believes the child's statement has enough *likelihood* of reliability to be worthy of being heard by the jury. Again, this exception to the general rule is intended to prevent trauma to a child victim.

As the criminal justice system becomes more concerned with the rights of child victims, however, it needs to continue to guard the rights of accused abusers as well. Two recent cases illustrate the tensions between the rights of child victims and the rights of people accused of child abuse.

In one case in Minnesota, members of six different families were accused of sexually abusing their own children and children related to them. The police removed children from the accused parents; scores of children were questioned by the police and prosecutors. Although these alleged acts occurred in a small town, every major television network reported the cases on their national news program. Locally and nationally the accused adults were branded as animals and worse.

However, all of the cases collapsed. One husband and wife were tried and acquitted while charges against twenty-one other adults were dismissed by the prosecutor when a number of children confessed that their stories about abuse were not true. One couple had had their three young children removed from their custody by a court order on the basis of other children's stories, which turned out to be false, yet from February to December, the court had refused to let this couple or their psychologists see their children. The entire incident was based on the fabricated stories of a number of children.

How could this happen? How could the police, the prosecutors, and the courts make so many mistakes at one time? Remember that the child victims were encouraged to talk and were quite literally told that it was permissible to accuse their parents and other adults of sex crimes, a normal investigative practice with children who are reluctant to accuse their parents of any wrongdoing. Even when some of the children recanted, saying they had made up the stories, the investigators assumed that either they had begun to feel sorry for and miss their parents, or were frightened of the unknown consequences of their actions in court.

Not surprisingly, the parents and other adults in this case are suing the local county and other officials for hundreds of millions of dollars. These civil actions will probably be in the courts for years. What may also be around for years is the emotional injury to both the parents and children who were separated as a result of the false accusations; the trauma may affect all of the participants in this tragedy for the rest of their lives.

Did the Minnesota law enforcement officials cross that invisible line between convincing the child that it is permissible to accuse an adult and suggesting an incident that never occurred? Consider a second case reported at the same time.

In a western state, teachers and administrators at a day care center were accused of sexually molesting a number of children. The investigator discovered that for many years children attending the day care center had been abused as scores of older children reported earlier incidents of repeated sexual molestation.

The community—indeed, the entire nation—was shocked. "How could so many repeated acts of child abuse occur over such a long period of time without someone discovering it?" people asked.

If the same investigative techniques employed in the Minnesota case had not been used here, it is fair to say, the day care center scandal would not have been uncovered. Nonetheless, law enforcement officials must be especially sensitive to the danger of false accusation and avoid actually suggesting the crime to the child. This becomes all the more important when the traditional ways in which our criminal justice system tests credibility—cross-examination, confrontation, presence in the courtroom, etc.—are eliminated in favor of protecting the child victim.

·5·

Spouse Abuse

Giving legal advice to every spouse abuse victim who reads this chapter would be impossible. There are too many victims, and the laws of the fifty states vary so much. So do the victims. There are some basic rules, however, all spouse abuse victims should remember.

First and foremost, spouse abuse, one person hitting another, is against the law. Whether or not your local arrest statute requires that a police officer see the assault take place, assaults—even within family units—are a crime. Under some circumstances such assaults will be prosecuted, but only if they are reported.

Second, arresting a spouse is neither easy nor enjoyable but it may be important, particularly considering that many women who fail to report these assaults become murder victims or murderers of their spouse. And children who witness spouse abuse frequently become abusers or victims themselves, a most unhappy legacy for any parent to leave a child.

Third, short of intervention by law enforcement agencies, there are many civil legal remedies a battered spouse may use. Some of these, described below, require a lawyer; others do not. (How to find a lawyer is described in Chapter 2.) Almost every community has a domestic violence shelter that provides a place to stay and can direct a spouse abuse victim to both legal and medical help. If a shelter is not listed in your telephone directory, call the police department or the local court (the "family division" of the local court if there is one) to find one. The local prosecutor's office, particularly if there is a victim/witness assistance unit, may also have information.

If you are separated from your spouse, the chances are good that forced sexual intercourse will be treated as marital rape, a crime.

Finally, both the abuser and the victim may benefit from some kind of counseling, which also can be ordered by a court in lieu of prosecution if the abuser will not undergo counseling voluntarily. Counseling may give the victim a more objective view of the marriage and the family unit. The local domestic violence shelter will probably be able to suggest a counselor.

Spouse abuse victims must exercise their legal rights themselves. Without this first step, the cycle of violence will continue from one generation to the next.

Sadly, you have a much greater chance of being assaulted in your own home than anywhere else, and most likely by someone you know. In a recent year, 40 percent of female homicide victims were killed by members of their families or by their boyfriends. In fact, marriage may be dangerous; three widely respected surveys on the incidence of spouse abuse in the United States found a range of incidence from a low of 10 percent of all married couples, to a high of 50 percent. The survey with the largest sample reported spouse abuse in over 25 percent of all marriages. In Cleveland, the police in a nine-month period received fifteen thousand calls for help in domestic disturbance cases, approximately one call every twenty-five minutes. Without doubt physical assaults within marriage are one of this nation's most frequently committed crimes, but one of its least reported. In recent years, however, the police and other government agencies have turned increased attention to spouse abuse.

Who are the abusers? Recent surveys suggest that in married couples where both spouses are under the age of fifty, most abusers are husbands. Where both spouses are over fifty, and particularly if the husband has become infirm because of illness, the wife is more frequently the abuser, although in this group, husbands still commit a majority of the assaults.

Because men are more frequently the abusers and women the victims, throughout this chapter masculine pronouns are used for assailants, and feminine for victims. Gender neutrality would be more accurate but also more confusing.

Myths about spouse abuse abound, and one is that more police officers are killed every year answering calls in domestic quarrels than in any other type of crime. This is simply not true. Fewer police officers are killed while responding to a domestic violence call than for any other report of an assault by people known to each other. Trying to stop a fight in the local bar is considerably more dangerous.

Our nation's response to spouse abuse has always tended to ignore the criminal nature of the problem. Until very recently, victims had few, if any, legal rights or remedies. Times are now changing, but how did we get to the point where things had to change before spouse abuse was recognized for the terrible crime it is?

The Legal History

Much of our legal philosophy and some of our laws were inherited from our English ancestors through the early American colonists. To some extent, so was domestic violence. Under English law, a husband and wife were regarded as one person, but, unfortunately, the one person was the husband. An English legal commentator described it as "the very being or legal existence of the woman is suspended during the marriage." Small wonder then that throughout English history men were permitted to beat their wives, "chastisement," as it was called. In fact, as a matter of law, men were permitted to chastise their wives "in the same moderation that a man is allowed to correct his apprentices or children." Both quotations are from the highly respected legal commentator Sir William Blackstone.

The severity of permissible chastisement varied from time to time and place to place. Even when a husband exceeded permissible limits of wife beating, though, there was little or nothing a wife could do. For instance, in an 1831 English case, a wife sought but was denied a divorce when the court acknowledged that the husband's physical abuse of his wife exceeded permissible chastisement, but concluded that the sanctity of marriage was more important.

Slowly, very slowly the doctrine of permissible wife beating was repudiated. Maryland became the first state to pass a law specifically prohibiting wife beating in 1882, with a sentence of forty lashes with a whip, or one year in jail for convicted husbands. In 1874 the North Carolina Supreme Court reversed a long line of cases by holding that a man had no right to chastise his wife, at least not by inflicting physical injury. Throughout the latter half of the nineteenth century, so-called married women's acts and emancipation acts were passed in virtually every state, giving married women a separate legal identity and separate ownership of property.

Following the enactment of this legislation, courts could no longer apply antiquated theories of a woman's role to a case of spouse abuse, but they took a different tack: marriage, they held, was a private affair between a man, a woman, and God; the state, through its courts, had no authority to interfere in the relationship even in the face of an accusation of assault. This doctrine of noninterference can be seen in many court decisions during the first seventy years of the twentieth century.

The courts' reluctance to address these problems influenced the response of prosecutors and police. Prosecutors were reluctant to pursue spouse abuse cases, and the police were reluctant to arrest without the prosecutors' support. And both complained of the wife's frequent refusal to press charges.

But the most important reason spouse abuse was ignored for so long by the criminal justice system may be that women, who are most frequently the victims of spouse abuse, were employed very infrequently as police officers, prosecutors, and judges. Prior to 1970, almost without exception, these positions were filled by men, who are usually the abusers in such cases. It is reasonable to suspect, then, that the participants in the system may have been reluctant to treat spouse abuse as a crime because they identified with the abusers.

There has been a dramatic improvement during the past few years in law enforcement's response to the problems of spouse abuse, but one need not study history to find a reluctance by government officials to address the issue. In many cases in the last ten years victim advocates have sued police departments, prosecutors, and other government officials, asking the courts to order them to enforce spouse abuse laws. These court petitions typically contain affidavits from scores (and more) of complainants who asked for help in stopping the violence in their marriages but were told there was nothing the police or prosecutors could do. These officials have often agreed to respond to the concerns of the petitioners, but even today, hundreds of years after Blackstone said a woman essentially had no legal rights with respect to her husband, some law enforcement agencies refuse to interfere in a spouse abuse case.

The Present Law

During the last decade, every state has enacted legislation to address family violence, particularly domestic violence, an effort led for the most part by victim advocates from women's shelters and attorneys representing women in domestic relations cases. They have drafted legislation, presented data to legislative committees, and generally lobbied for change. Rarely has the impetus for change come from within a state legislature. Some changes affecting the rights of victims of spouse abuse have also come from court decisions.

Essentially, the expanding legal rights of spouse abuse victims have been of two types: rights providing for civil remedies meant to stop the violence, and rights permitting or even requiring specific responses by law enforcement authorities to reports of spouse abuse. Civil remedies provide for many flexible forms of relief, while criminal remedies are available only through the cooperation of police and prosecutors and can result only in imprisonment, probation, fines, or forced counseling for the offender.

Civil Remedies
With only one exception, every state has enacted legislation permitting courts to alter the living arrangements and

economic conditions within a marriage in order to prevent violence. For instance, courts can order a spouse to refrain from violence. Admittedly, a court order is only a piece of paper, which some are prepared to ignore, but most judges are ready to invoke sanctions, including fines and jail, against an offender.

In most jurisdictions, this protective order or restraining order orders the abuser to have no further contact with the victim, to refrain from verbal threats, to support the victim (and children, if any), and to pay court costs and attorney's fees.

One of the most effective ways of halting abuse is to order the abuser to leave his residence. Approximately 75 percent of the states have legislation permitting this, and in many jurisdictions it can be accomplished even if the title to the house or the lease of rental property is in the abuser's name. In many states, the order requiring the abuser to leave can be entered following an *ex parte* hearing, one at which the abuser is neither present nor represented by a lawyer.

This sounds fairly severe—throwing a person out of his house following a secret court hearing in which he is not present—but such laws have been challenged on constitutional grounds and, without exception, upheld. In the first case involving such a challenge the Missouri Supreme Court considered a woman who had applied to a lower court for an order that required her husband to leave their home, an "order of eviction," as it is typically called. The lower court had granted the order following an *ex parte* hearing.

The alleged abuser, a 6-foot-4-inch, 250-pound, former Golden Gloves boxer, had been married to the victim for several years. She claimed her husband had assaulted her on many occasions, the last being so severe she had to be hospitalized for nine days. She left the hospital and, without returning home, went to the court for an order of eviction.

In upholding the order of eviction, and the statute which

permitted it, the Missouri Supreme Court found that the statute provided the only alternative available to the victim other than abandoning her house or risking further injury or death. Under this statute, the evicted person could return to court within a few days—most state statutes say three to five days—for a full hearing at which he could be represented by counsel and could testify. If the order of eviction was unfair, it could then be set aside. The rights of the victim, the court found, indeed the life of the victim, could be protected only through the order of eviction, but the rights of the alleged abuser, while temporarily reduced in favor of the victim's, could receive full consideration a few days after the eviction. Thus the order was upheld.

In some states, instead of ordering the alleged abuser out of the marital home, a court can require him to pay for alternative housing for the victim pending a court hearing. During this hearing, courts can also determine, in some states, temporary custody of minor children and the disposition of personal property. Almost everywhere, courts can order the abuser to pay court costs and attorneys' fees.

In some states courts can order almost any reasonable act to protect a victim and her property. Of course, in many states, all of the civil remedies can be altered by a separation agreement or by a divorce decree. However, even without these, the court orders described here can require one party or the other to do specific things for a long period of time, or until the court sets aside the order.

Although they are not strictly civil remedies, many state statutes require two other things. First, because for many years there was a lack of data about the incidents and severity of spouse abuse, making it very difficult to know what laws were needed, most statutes now require a state agency to keep records about reports of spouse abuse. These records give law enforcement agencies, social service professionals, the legislature, the courts, and others an accurate picture of spouse abuse.

Second, most states have separate funding for spouse abuse shelters, where victims and their children can live for a period of time, and for other services like counseling, job training and testing, and legal assistance. In approximately twenty states, the funds for spouse abuse services come from a surcharge on marriage licenses.

While these remedies are effective, their availability is sometimes limited by strict eligibility requirements. For instance, in many states, civil remedies are denied to victims who are not presently living with the abuser. In one study of women who required medical treatment following abuse, over one-half were divorced from, separated from, or not legally married to their assailant, and thus were ineligible for civil remedy protection. In fact, in a few states, even if a man and woman are living together and have children, civil remedies are unavailable to a victim without proof of a legal marriage.

Psychological abuse or harassment is not included among those "assaults" for which a civil remedy is available. Physical touching is required before a victim may apply for an order of protection.

Criminal Law Remedies

In many states, regardless of the crimes, police may not arrest unless a felony has been committed and the police have probable cause to believe a particular person committed the felony or a misdemeanor has been committed in the officer's presence. It is not enough for the officer to believe a misdemeanor has been committed, even if the evidence is overwhelming; the officer must have actually seen it.

A misdemeanor is less serious than a felony. In many

states, it has a maximum punishment of one year or less in jail while a felony carries more than a year. In most states, for an assault to be a felony, it must be committed with a gun or a knife, or else the victim must have suffered "grievous bodily harm."

By these definitions, most incidents of spouse abuse are misdemeanors. The police are powerless to make an arrest in a domestic fight unless they see the assault happen, which is unlikely, or the assault is a felony. Combining police discretion not to make an arrest in every case—a discretion we would not want to eliminate—and the reluctance of many police officers to get involved in spouse abuse cases makes it unsurprising that lawsuits have been brought to force the police to arrest in spouse abuse cases. Police officers, as a group, appear to be involved in a higher percentage of spouse abuse cases themselves than almost any other professional group (or so some studies indicate), so they may not be the most appropriate people to respond to these problems.

Many states, through legislation, have expanded the authority of police officers to arrest in spouse abuse cases. Typically, this legislation creates an exception to the usual misdemeanor assault rule by allowing an arrest even if the assault was not committed in the officer's presence. In addition, if a court has issued a protective order, and the police officer has probable cause to believe it has been violated, the officer may make an arrest. Over half the states have enacted this sort of legislation.

A few states have gone further; if a police officer knows spouse abuse has been committed, the officer must make an arrest; there is no discretion. One state court has even held that a police officer who must make an arrest (in accordance with a statute) in a spouse abuse case and fails to do so is subject to a lawsuit by the victim.

During the past few years, there has been extensive publicity about the effectiveness of arrest in stopping spouse abuse. A government-funded study examined differing responses to complaints of spouse abuse in Minneapolis during 1981 and 1982. In the study, in misdemeanor cases between family members, where there was no severe injury, the police undertook on a random basis one of three actions: arrest, removal from the home for a cooling off period, or advice and counseling by the police.

In 35 percent of the cases in which there was no arrest, victims reported at least one additional incident of violence within six months. But in arrest cases, only 19 percent of the victims reported another incident of violence. Although not officially part of the experiment, it is worth noting that of the 136 arrests that were made, only 3 led to convictions. To some extent, therefore, it seems arrest acted as a deterrent regardless of what happened to the case in court. Despite the results of this study—and the wide publicity it was given—it should be noted that the results are directly contrary to those of another study done at the same time in a different city, which showed no connection between incidents of additional domestic violence and arrest. Of the 314 cases in the Minneapolis study, most were unmarried or minority or mixed-race couples living together, with a very low employment rate, a large percentage of whom had criminal records. Spouse abuse, on the other hand, occurs in all economic classes and races. In fact, one national study reported the greatest number of spouse abuse cases occur in people with a seventh- to ninth-grade education level, and the second most frequent occurs in people with a post-college degree. And well-educated victims are the least likely to report spouse abuse.

Some states require police officers to transport victims of spouse abuse to the closest shelter or temporary housing facility, and some laws require police to explain to the victim what her legal options are, including the right to a protective order.

Prosecutor's offices do not have to prosecute all spouse abuse cases but some offices have shown a greater willingness to prosecute spouse abuse cases than was typical just a few years ago. In addition to establishing special prosecution units for all family violence cases, some prosecutors have started special victim units to give support to spouse abuse victims and to encourage them to prosecute. (These are discussed in Chapter 1.) In some prosecutors' offices, victim advocates review reports of police responses to domestic violence calls where an arrest was not made and contact the victim to determine whether prosecution would still be appropriate.

Unfortunately in many parts of the country, prosecutors continue to treat spouse abuse as though it were not a crime, viewing intrafamily assaults as different from other assaults.

Some jurisdictions have responded to spouse abuse cases by creating special courts for the resolution of all domestic violence matters. Chicago has such a court. In at least one state, legislation has been passed that requires a judge to sentence a convicted spouse abuser to some period of time in prison. There is no discretion; if the person is convicted he must go to prison.

In some states, however, a spouse abuse conviction will not result in a prison term, but in a period of probation. As a condition of probation, the court may order counseling for the abuser. In addition, abusers are sometimes directed to a counseling program in lieu of prosecution. If the abuser successfully completes the program, the case is dismissed. But abuser counseling has caused some controversy about what is best for the victim.

For many years there has been extensive counseling for victims. Frequently, spouse abuse continues because the wife lacks the economic resources to break away from the marriage, has to care for her children, and may lack the self-esteem needed to end a relationship doomed by the faults of another person. Particularly when many young married people, because of job or education commitments, live far away from the family and friends they grew up with, many young women are without the support that could help if they were in familiar surroundings.

Shelters for battered women provide a resource for the abused spouse. It is a place to live at nominal or no cost, it provides at least temporary shelter for children, it is staffed by victim advocates who can advise a woman on her options, both civil and criminal, and it can direct a woman to other services such as legal counseling. A shelter also can be a place for companionship and support. Most of all, a shelter can give or direct a victim to counseling services. All victims suffer at least some emotional shock, but victims of spouse abuse, especially because it frequently lasts over a long period of time, have special problems. Counseling is very important for such victims.

Some states fund spouse abuse services, but, without exception, these funds are both limited and insufficient, and the resources spread very thin. Therefore, any program that counsels abusers, drawing away funds from victim services, will be viewed with suspicion or worse by some victim advocates.

The question remains: what will benefit the victim the most? The answer is both—counseling for the victim and for the abuser. Evidence shows that abuser counseling programs do a lot more to diminish and even eliminate abuse than any other available service. At least one study of over one hundred men arrested for spouse abuse and ordered to a counseling program in lieu of prosecution reported a 100 percent success rate; not one single man who completed the program assaulted his spouse again, at least not during the period of the study. While that is an unusual success rate—perhaps even phenomenal—other studies of these programs reflect results almost as good.

Abuser counseling should not replace victim counseling, but neither should victim counseling exist to the exclusion of abuser counseling. When one considers the cycle of violence associated with spouse abuse, abuser counseling appears to be an extremely effective means of breaking the cycle, preventing spouse abuse in the future.

Battered Spouse Syndrome

Sometimes spouse abuse leads to the homicide of the abuser. Every year, scores of women charged with murdering their husbands attempt to defend themselves in criminal court through a plea of self-defense. Controversy has arisen over whether testimony should be introduced to show that the wife suffers from "battered spouse syndrome," a term used to describe a set of symptoms psychologists found common to many spouse abuse cases. If a woman has these symptoms, which result from repeated beatings, she must have suffered repeated beatings. Some courts claim battered spouse syndrome has not gained sufficient professional acceptance to be introduced into a trial.

Obviously, any testimony that shows a defendant suffers from this syndrome tends to support a self-defense claim when the defendant is charged with killing her spouse. However, courts will not allow scientific evidence unless the scientific community generally recognizes the validity of the science or data involved. Not all scientists believe the battered spouse syndrome exists, and thus not all courts admit testimony about it.

For instance, a trial court in Illinois refused to admit evidence of battered spouse syndrome when a wife claimed self-defense in an answer to a murder charge. She was convicted. On appeal, however, the Illinois Supreme Court ordered a new trial and granted the woman the opportunity to introduce this evidence. In approximately half the states, courts have admitted expert testimony concerning the syndrome.

There can be little doubt, however, that some women are forced to fight for their lives within their marriages. During each of the past five years, over four thousand women per year were beaten to death by their husbands.

Marital Rape

Spouse abuse can take many forms. However, it is not clear that the criminal justice system will interfere with forced sexual intercourse between husband and wife.

The legal rights of sexual assault victims are discussed in Chapter 6. Despite criminal law's reluctance to recognize it as such, though, it seems clear that marital rape is a crime, but one for which victims have few rights.

It is not surprising that a legal system that once permitted men to beat their wives still believes a man cannot be prosecuted for raping his wife. Other arguments against marital rape laws are also frequently heard. For instance, some commentators have stated that marriage constitutes blanket consent by a woman to sexual intercourse with her husband, and others state that intercourse between a husband and wife is always lawful, unlike rape. Finally, some argue that a marital rape law would discourage harmony in the family and lead to more divorces.

Whatever the reason, almost without exception, sexual assault criminal statutes define rape as sexual intercourse between a man and a woman "not his wife," and define sexual assault as sexual contact between a person and another "not his spouse." Interestingly, these same laws do not allow a husband to procure or aid another man to have sexual intercourse with his wife.

In Massachusetts, New Jersey, New York, Virginia, and

Georgia, courts have upheld the arrest and conviction of a husband for raping his wife. In some of these, the husbands were separated and estranged from their wives and not actually living with them. The courts held the marriage had actually—if not legally—ended. But courts in twenty-three states have held that a husband cannot be convicted of raping his wife.

Decisions like these may make us wonder if we have come very far since Blackstone's era.

But spouse abuse—physical violence by one spouse against another—is a crime. It should be reported. If it is not, children of the marriage are likely to become either abusers or victims of abuse. More importantly, in almost all states, there are public and private organizations that can help the victim to escape from the abusive relationship and begin a new life. A partial list of domestic violence shelters and other organizations throughout the country appears at the end of this chapter. These organizations can offer a great deal of help.

DOMESTIC VIOLENCE SHELTERS BY STATE

Alabama Coalition Against
Domestic Violence
Safeplace, Inc.
P.O. Box 1456
Florence, AL 35630
(205) 767-6210

Alaska Network on Domestic
Violence and Sexual Assault
110 Seward Street #13
Juneau, AK 99801
(907) 586-3650

Arizona Coalition Against
Domestic Violence
P.O. Box 27365
Tempe, AZ 85282
(602) 234-4402

Arkansas Coalition Against
Violence to Women and
Children
P.O. Box 807
Harrison, AR 72601
(501) 741-6167

Central California Coalition
Against Domestic Violence
P.O. Box 3931
Modesto, CA 95352
(209) 575-7037

Northern California Shelter
Support Services
P.O. Box 1955
San Mateo, CA 94401
(415) 342-0850

Southern California Coalition on
Battered Women
P.O. Box 5036
Santa Monica, CA 90405
(213) 392-9874

Colorado Domestic Violence
Coalition
P.O. Box 18902
Denver, CO 80218
(303) 394-2810

Task Force on Abused Women
P.O. Box 14299
Hartford, CT 06106
(203) 524-5890

Delaware Commission for
Women
Department of Community
Education
Carval State Building
820 North French Street
Wilmington, DE 19801
(302) 571-2660

My Sister's Place
P.O. Box 29596
Washington, D.C. 20017-0796
(202) 529-5991 (Hotline)

Refuge Information Network of
Florida
c/o Women in Distress
P.O. Box 676
Fort Lauderdale, FL 33302
1-800-342-9152 (Hotline)

Georgia Network Against
Domestic Violence
P.O. Box 22487
Savannah, GA 31403
(912) 234-9999

Shelter for Abused Spouses and
Children
200 North Vineyard Blvd. #20
Honolulu, HI 96817
(808) 841-0822 (Hotline)

Idaho Council on Family
Violence
450 West State Street
Statehouse Mail, 10th Fl.
Boise, ID 83720
(208) 334-4171

Illinois Coalition Against
Domestic Violence
931 South Fourth Street
Springfield, IL 62704
1-800-252-6561 (Hotline)

Indiana Coalition Against
Domestic Violence
919 East Second Street
Bloomington, IN 47401
(812) 334-8378

Family Violence Center
1101 Walnut Street
Des Moines, IA 50309
(515) 243-6147

Domestic Violence Task Force
Route 1, Box 73
Atchinson, KS 66002
(919) 367-5345

Kentucky Domestic Violence
Association
Women's Crisis Center
321 York Street
Newport, KY 41071
(502) 581-7222 (Hotline)

Louisiana Coalition Against
Domestic Violence
c/o Crescent House
1231 Prytania Street
New Orleans, LA 70130
(504) 523-3755

Maine Coalition for Family
Crisis Services
P.O. Box 304
Augusta, ME 04861
(207) 623-3569

Maryland Network Against
Domestic Violence
2427 Maryland Avenue
Baltimore, MD 21218
(301) 268-4393

Massachusetts Coalition of
Battered Women's Service
Groups
25 West Street, 5th Fl.
Boston, MA 02111
(617) 423-7944

YWCA Domestic Violence
Services
310 E. Third Street
Flint, MI 48502
(313) 238-7621

Minnesota Coalition for
Battered Women
435 Aldine Street
St. Paul, MN 55104
(612) 646-6177

Mississippi Coalition Against
Domestic Violence
P.O. Box 333
Biloxi, MS 39533

Missouri Coalition Against
Domestic Violence
27 North Newstead
St. Louis, MO 63108
(314) 531-2005

Montana Coalition Against
Domestic Violence
P.O. Box 6183
Great Falls, MT 59406
(406) 228-4435

Nebraska Task Force on
Domestic Violence & Sexual
Assault
YWCA
222 South 29th Street
Omaha, NE 68131
(402) 345-7273

Assistance for Domestic Crisis
P.O. Box 43264
Las Vegas, NV 89116
(702) 646-4981

New Hampshire Coalition
Against Family Violence
P.O. Box 353
Concord, NH 03301
1-800-852-3311 (Hotline)

New Jersey Coalition for
Battered Women
206 West State Street
Trenton, NJ 08608
1-800-322-8092 (Hotline)

Shelter for Victims of Domestic
Violence
P.O. Box 336
Albuquerque, NM 87103
(505) 247-4219

New York State Coalition
Against Domestic Violence
5 Neher Street
Woodstock, NY 12498
1-800-942-6906 (Hotline)

North Carolina Association of
Domestic Violence Programs
P.O. Box 595
Wilmington, NC 28402
(919) 343-0703

North Dakota Council on
Abused Women's Services
311 Thayer, Room 127
Bismarck, ND 58501
(701) 255-6240

Action for Battered Women
P.O. Box 2421
Youngstown, OH 44509
(216) 793-3363

Domestic Violence Intervention
Services
1331 E. 15th Street
Tulsa, OK 74120
(918) 585-3143

Oregon Coalition Against
Domestic & Sexual Violence
2336 S.E. Belmont Street
Portland, OR 97214
(503) 239-4486

Pennsylvania Coalition Against
Domestic Violence
2250 Elmerton Avenue
Harrisburg, PA 17110
(717) 652-9571

Battered Women's Shelter
Casa Julia de Burgos
P.O. Box 2433
San Juan, Puerto Rico 00936

Rhode Island Council on
Domestic Violence
P.O. Box 1829
Providence, RI 02912
(401) 272-9524

South Carolina Coalition
Against Domestic Violence &
Sexual Assault
P.O. Box 7291
Columbia, SC 29202

South Dakota Coalition Against
Domestic Violence
Resource Center for Women
317 South Kline
Aberdeen, SD 57401
(605) 226-1212

Tennessee Coalition Against
Domestic Violence
P.O. Box 831
Newport, TN 37821
(615) 623-3125

Texas Council on Family
Violence
509-A West Lynn
Austin, TX 78746
(512) 482-8200

Utah Domestic Violence
Council
c/o Division of Family Services
150 West North Temple
Salt Lake City, UT 84103

Vermont Domestic Violence
Programs
Herstory House Shelter
P.O. Box 313
Rutland, VT 05701
(802) 775-3232 (Hotline)

Virginians Against Domestic
Violence
P.O. Box 5692
Richmond, VA 23220
(703) 532-3175

Washington State Shelter
Network
1063 S., Capital Way #217
Olympia, WA 98501
(206) 753-4621

Task Force on Domestic
Violence
P.O. Box 626
Fairmont, WV 26554
(304) 367-1100

Milwaukee Women's Refuge
P.O. Box 11443
Milwaukee, WI 53211
(414) 671-6140

Wyoming Coalition on Family
Violence & Sexual Assault
P.O. Box 1127
Riverton, WY 82501
(307) 856-0942

·6·

Sexual Assault

Rape! There is something frightening about that word. It describes an act far more horrible than most other crimes. Rape deprives many victims of their dignity, their self-worth, their compassion, and most of all their humanity.

Before describing the legal rights of victims of sexual assault, we should mention some nonlegal ones. Victims of sexual assault should have a medical examination. There are some legal issues associated with such an examination, which will be described later, but victims should remember that physical injury is usually best treated by a physician and that most venereal diseases are detectable and treatable. Victims may also need the help of a rape counselor or other professional to help with problems induced by the assault. However, many victims have no postassault disorders, and in one well-known research project, one-quarter of the rape victims did not suffer from any such disorders.

Some victims are moderately or severely depressed following the rape, and others continue to suffer from psychological problems for a year or more. The major difficulties are fear and anxiety, with some victims also experiencing flashbacks or concern about social censure. Not surprisingly, many rape victims suffer from sexual dysfunction afterward. And, sadly, a large percentage of all women who attempt suicide have been rape victims.

In short, sexual assault victims may need counseling of some kind immediately following the assault, and perhaps for some period thereafter. In most areas, rape crisis centers offer counseling, as do psychologists, psychiatrists or other mental health care professionals. Victims should be encouraged to seek this help. See the end of this chapter for a list of rape crisis centers.

Rape is a vastly underreported crime. The decision to report or not, which has important legal consequences, is one a victim may wish to make after consulting with others. In many states, statements made to a rape counselor or a lawyer are confidential and may not be disclosed without the permission of the victim.

If a victim is reluctant to report a rape because she fears her reputation will be put on trial, inform her of the rape shield laws, described below, that exist in most states. If her reluctance is based on the necessity of a gynecological examination, inform her of the procedures, described below, used in such examinations, which might be needed solely for health reasons, as well.

The sooner a physical examination is made, the greater the possibility there will be at least some corroboration of the sexual assault. And the more rapidly a rape is reported, the better the chances of the police catching the assailant. As noted in Chapter 3, reporting a rape can also allow the victim to sue the assailant in civil court and receive money damages.

The identity of a rape victim might be reported in the news, but most media representatives exercise self-restraint in this area. Those who do not face the prospect of being sued by victims whose names are revealed. In many states, a sexual assault victim may keep her privacy by testifying about the sexual assault in a courtroom that has been locked to all but essential court personnel.

Many communities have a rape crisis center, which can be of tremendous assistance. Not only do rape crisis counselors provide information about the criminal justice system, but they can also offer companionship and compassion when both qualities are desperately needed. And rape crisis counselors have been responsible for many of the legal reforms that have benefited victims of all crimes.

There are many rape victims; in fact there are so many, it is difficult to determine the number. In 1983, the latest year for which we have statistics, there were 99,000 cases of rape *reported* to the police, and everyone agrees many more go unreported. How many more is an open question. The United States Department of Justice estimates that 56 percent of all rapes get reported, meaning over 177,000 rapes were actually committed in 1983, one every three minutes. But there were clearly many more rapes in 1983. Victimization surveys conducted by the Federal Bureau of Investigation, the Census Bureau, and the National Opinion Research Center report that only between 3.5 percent and 10 percent of all rapes are actually reported.

There are two kinds of rapes in law, unlawful sexual intercourse with a woman against her will by force or threat of force, and statutory rape, which is sexual intercourse with a female under a particular age, usually fifteen or sixteen, depending on the state. (For a discussion of marital rape, see Chapter 5.)

In most states, the term "sexual intercourse" means penile-vaginal contact; any penetration fulfills the legal requirements of rape. If the victim is a virgin, breaking of the hymen is not required, and in no state is it necessary for there to have been an emission of sperm for rape to have taken place.

Some rape cases turn on the legal question of whether sexual intercourse was "against the will" of the victim. Entire books have been written on the subject of when, and how, and to what extent a woman must resist an attempt to commit sexual intercourse. A jury can convict a rapist only if there was some resistance. While different jurisdictions have different rules about this, there are some common themes. First, there must be some resistance in the usual sense of that word. The response, "I don't think so," to an invitation to sexual intercourse—in the absence of a weapon or threats—is not resistance. By act or deed or affirmative statement, there must be a clear signal on the part of the woman that she is not willing to have sexual intercourse. This does not mean the victim must hit the man, or try to flee, or even scream, and in the face of overwhelming force—such as a weapon—she does not have to risk her life or serious injury with some futile act of resistance. Even without a weapon, the force can be overwhelming through the use of physical threats or intimidation.

The issue of consent—frequently the basis of a defense—requires the jury or the judge when there is no jury to look into the minds of the defendant and the victim, a very difficult assignment. Sometimes there is helpful evidence such as the defendant being arrested on the scene with a loaded gun in his hand, or injuries suffered by the victim.

But where there is a lack of evidence for either the defendant's story or the victim's, the jury must weigh their stories, and try to determine which is true. The law is clear: if the defendant reasonably believed the victim was consenting to sexual intercourse, he is not guilty because he did not intend to commit a crime. Of course, his belief must be a reasonable one; if it isn't he can be found guilty of rape, and his mistaken, unreasonable belief is an insufficient defense.

Rape can and frequently does occur on a date or other social occasion. The question of consent in such cases is sometimes a difficult one. However, rape is against the law regardless of whether the defendant and the victim are acquainted or are in a social setting. Some surveys suggest a woman has a far greater chance of being raped by someone she knows than by a stranger. In such cases the defendant frequently claims consent. When that happens, the promptness with which the victim reported the rape to the police becomes a crucial factor; if you want to prosecute, report the rape as soon as possible.

Frequently, social companion sexual assault takes place in educational settings. A 1985 study at a coeducational eastern university found that 76 percent of the female students had been sexually harassed at least once during the past five years. Harassment was defined as "(a) unwanted teasing, remarks, or gestures; (b) unwanted pressure for dates; and (c) unwanted deliberate touching, leaning over, cornering, or pinching, as well as actual or attempted rape or sexual assault."

Sexual intercourse with a woman who has not attained "the age of consent" is statutory rape. In some states the victim must be below the age of puberty to be a victim of statutory rape, but in most states there is a specific age, usually fifteen or sixteen. Essentially, the law states that a woman below the age of consent is too young to give consent, and therefore, anyone who has sexual intercourse with her is committing rape. In most states, mentally impaired women are protected under the same statute.

Statutory rape in most states is a strict liability crime, meaning that an honest and reasonable mistake about the age of the woman is not a defense. Where the age of consent is sixteen, sexual intercourse with a fifteen-year-old who looks twenty-two and has identification showing she is that age is still statutory rape. Some states have softened this strict liability rule.

Rape is not the only sexual assault. In all states forced sexual contact between homosexuals is against the law, as is forced heterosexual contact with a body cavity other than the vagina. This crime is frequently called sodomy. (Sexual contact involving child victims is discussed in Chapter 4.)

Rape Shield Laws

Assume you were on a jury trying to decide if Smith killed Jones in cold blood, as charged by the prosecutor, or in self-defense, as claimed by Smith. The killing took place in a bar following an argument between the two men, but the eyewitness testimony was contradictory, some favoring Jones and the others Smith. Would you want to know if Smith had a reputation for starting fights in the past? How about Jones?

If the answer is yes, change the facts and assume Smith is charged with raping Jones. Smith claims consent, while Jones claims she resisted but was overpowered. The other evidence in the case is inconclusive. Would you, as a juror, want to know whether Jones had accused other men of rape? Would you want to know whether Smith had previously been convicted of rape? Would it be important for you to know if the two had sexual intercourse by consent before the rape?

Ordinarily, in a criminal trial, the law forbids the introduction of character evidence to prove or establish conduct. There are, however, exceptions to this general rule. In murder cases, for instance, when there is an issue of self-defense, the defense may introduce evidence about the victim's reputation for violent behavior, and the prosecution can then introduce evidence about the victim's reputation for nonviolent behavior. In most jurisdictions, the same rule applies to assault cases.

What if in a rape case the defendant claims the victim consented to the act of sexual intercourse? Should the defense attorney have the right to cross-examine the victim by asking questions such as:

"Is it true you and the defendant had sexual intercourse at least five times before you reported rape on the sixth?

"Is it true you have had sexual intercourse with four other men?

"Is it true you consented to sexual intercourse on this occasion and every other occasion during your life?"

Historically, the law permitted the defense to challenge the victim's reputation for chastity through cross-examination and sometimes through direct evidence, i.e., calling as witnesses men who claimed they had had sexual intercourse with the victim. Thereafter, and sometimes in anticipation of such evidence, the prosecution could present favorable evidence about the victim's reputation for chastity.

That has all changed. Nearly every jurisdiction has enacted "rape shield laws" that either forbid evidence concerning the chastity of the victim or (in a few states) require a preliminary hearing for the purpose of strictly limiting or screening out this evidence. The Federal Rules of Evidence used in federal courts are typical of such laws, forbidding evidence about past sexual activity unless certain conditions are met. First, this evidence can only be introduced on the question of consent. Second, if the victim says she was injured during the rape, or if the evidence shows the presence of semen, the defendant may try to prove that other men (or events) are the source of the injury or the semen. In some states, neither of these exceptions exists, and all evidence about a victim's sexual reputation is inadmissible.

An interesting feature of the Federal Rules of Evidence and of some state rules is that if this evidence is going to be introduced at trial, a special, pretrial evidentiary hearing is conducted with the victim present if she chooses, at which the trial judge determines whether the evidence the accused seeks to offer is relevant and that the value of such evidence to help the fact finder reach a verdict outweighs the danger of unfair prejudice to the victim.

Shortly after the first rape shield laws were enacted, they were challenged on the grounds they interfered with the defendant's right to confront an accuser, the so-called confrontation clause contained in the sixth amendment to the United States Constitution. The courts held that most evidence about a victim's chastity has little or no value on the issue of consent. In addition, the courts weighed the embarrassment to the victim when such evidence is offered against the rights of the defendant, and almost unanimously decided in favor of the victim.

Evidence of Sexual Assault

When a rape is promptly reported, law enforcement officials should arrange for a gynecological examination of the victim to determine whether there is evidence of forced sexual intercourse. In addition, sometimes hair or blood samples of the assailant can be discovered during these examinations.

Until a few years ago, rape victims were taken to a local hospital where personnel who were medically but not legally trained conducted the examination. Obviously, this is a very personal examination, frequently performed in an emergency room and not always in private. Until recently, they might be done with police officers present, and the rape victim was usually not permitted to have friends or relatives present. Often, despite the fact that the police had requested the examination, the victim had to pay for it. Sometimes the evidence was improperly collected or overlooked altogether because the medical personnel did not understand the significance of what they found as evidence. Professionals who could treat the nonphysical injuries of the victim were frequently unavailable.

Recently, in most (but not all) states, these examinations have improved significantly. Medical personnel are now, for the most part, trained about the evidentiary importance of the examination, usually by rape crisis center counselors or other victim advocates. The psychological needs of rape victims are better understood as well, and counseling services are offered to the victims, sometimes through referral to a rape crisis center. A rape crisis counselor is usually permitted in the examining room with the victim, which can go a long way toward alleviating fears and doubts.

The need for privacy in such examinations is now understood. Almost everywhere, the victim is no longer forced to pay for what is essentially a law enforcement responsibility. Male police officers are excluded from the examining rooms. Additionally, the police have been instructed that because of the trauma associated with rape, prompt questioning of the victim is medically unsound; if the victim is given some time to recover from the assault before being questioned, more useful information—from a law enforcement standpoint—may be forthcoming. More women police officers are assigned to investigate rape cases, and many police forces are forming special rape squads with special training to investigate sexual assault cases.

Corroboration

Essentially a corroboration rule requires the prosecutor to present to the jury some evidence that supports the victim's accusations. The corroboration can take many forms, including an eyewitness to the rape, the mental or physical condition of the victim immediately following the rape, a prompt report to the police or family and friends, the condition of the victim's clothing immediately following the rape, and the condition of the accused immediately following the rape. The amount of corroboration required need not be so great that, by itself, it would convict the accused, but it should prove the rape occurred as testified to by the victim.

Although we can blame our English law heritage on the existence of some rules detrimental to victims' rights, the rule of corroboration is of our own making. Certain states, either by passing laws to this effect or by court decisions, have decided that some corroboration of the rape victim's testimony is required, even though they have no such requirement for any other assault. They argue that corroboration will prevent false accusations of rape, balance the defendant's rights with the prosecution's rights because it is easy for the prosecutor to obtain a conviction for rape, and balance the sympathy the jury will feel for the victim. Of course, the substantial underreporting of rape offenses tends to refute the false accusations argument, and there is no evidence that juries are more sympathetic to rape victims or that prosecutors win these cases more frequently.

The need for corroboration is not the same in every state, nor is it the same in every type of case. In some states corroboration is not required if the victim's story is clear and convincing enough by itself to support a conviction. Obviously, an articulate rape victim here has a decided advantage over an inarticulate one. In other states, corroboration is not required where the victim is "mature," usually defined as being over the age of consent, or has made a prompt report to the police. Thus corroboration is not required except in statutory rape cases or when the report of rape was not promptly made. Finally, in a few states, corroboration is required in all rape cases, and in all other sexual assault cases.

Privacy of the Rape Victim

Approximately ten years ago, a young woman was raped and murdered in Georgia. A television news reporter obtained her name from official court records and reported it on a television newscast. The father of the victim brought an action for invasion of privacy, basing his case on a Georgia criminal statute that makes it a misdemeanor to publish the identity of a rape victim.

This case was appealed to the United States Supreme Court, which held that the statute violated the free press guarantee of the First Amendment insofar as it made it a crime to publish names contained in court records. The Supreme Court, however, did not hold that a criminal statute prohibiting the publication of the name of a rape victim is unconstitutional if the name of the victim is obtained from a source other than public record, nor did the court hold that an invasion of privacy action may not be brought when a news media institution reveals the identity of a rape victim. In fact, the California Supreme Court has held that the publication of a rape victim's identity is an invasion of privacy for which the victim can recover damages.

Invasion of privacy as the basis of a lawsuit is a difficult legal issue to describe, and equally difficult to win. Generally, a victim may win an invasion of privacy suit if she can prove the publication concerns a private matter that was unknown to the public, the matter is highly offensive, and the matter is not of legitimate concern to the public. The first two requirements are not difficult to establish. It is the third that causes the greatest number of rape victims to forego an invasion of privacy suit. What one judge or jury sees as legitimate concern to the public another may decide is not the public's business. It is virtually impossible to predict what a court or jury will do in such a case. The fact that many journalists routinely omit the names of sexual assault victims from their stories may help to establish that at least some members of the news media do not consider the victim's identity to be among the legitimate concerns of the public.

Privacy

The Sixth Amendment to the United States Constitution guarantees a defendant in a criminal case the right to a public trial. This same provision exists in most state constitutions, and sometimes in state rules of criminal procedure. Notwithstanding this provision or rule, some courts have at times excluded the public from all trials, including rape and other sexual assault cases. In some states, for some trials, exclusion of the public is required.

A number of courts have upheld the constitutionality of these exclusion rules, as long as those people who have a direct interest in the case can be present. "Direct interest" people include the parties, their lawyers, close relatives and friends of the parties, representatives of the press, and court personnel.

While a rape victim might ask that the public be excluded from a trial, or at least excluded during her testimony, there is a related problem about the right of the victim herself to be present at the trial. Almost without exception, witnesses at a trial cannot be present in the courtroom before they testify. Such a rule prevents one witness from hearing another's version of the facts. But what happens when the witness has finished testifying?

Frequently, in rape cases, defense counsel will request that the victim be forbidden to remain in the courtroom after she has testifed on the theory that the less the jury sees of the victim, the better for the defendant. Of course, the Sixth Amendment guarantees the right of the defendant to be present in court at all times.

Unfortunately, there is no similar guarantee for the rape victim, or any other victim of any other crime. Some judges require all witnesses to remain outside the court both before and after they have testified. However, if you are a victim in a sexual assault case or any other case, ask the judge if you can remain in the courtroom after you have testified or else have the prosecutor ask the judge on your behalf. You have a direct interest in the outcome of the case, so do not be reluctant to speak up for your rights.

The Privacy of Communications with Rape Crisis Counselors

Twenty years ago there were very few, if any, rape crisis centers. Today, there are well over six hundred, and most cities and densely populated counties have at least one or more such centers; names and telephone numbers of at least one rape crisis center per state are listed at the end of this chapter. Thousands of full-time and part-time rape crisis counselors work in these centers; many are unpaid volunteers.

As noted above, both health care professionals and courts recognize the role of the rape counselor in providing support and companionship for victims. Police and prosecutors usually work closely with the counselors and other staff of rape crisis centers. More importantly, for many victims these counselors perform an invaluable service as counselor, friend, companion, and buffer between the victim and the criminal justice system.

But what about the conversations between a rape counselor and a victim? Can a defense attorney force the counselor to reveal in court what the victim said about the sexual assault? Can the defense lawyer force the rape crisis center to turn over files that concern the sexual assault with which the defendant is charged?

If you find yourself saying "of course not!", consider a case in which the sexual assault victim testifies in court, under oath, that the defendant assaulted her, but tells the counselor in private she is not sure at all if the defendant is the person who assaulted her. What if she testifies in court she was sexually assaulted, but tells the counselor she actually consented?

During the past few years, the confidentiality of statements made by victims to rape counselors and the records of rape counselors have been the focus of extensive litigation and legislative action. Twelve states have enacted legislation that provides some protection for victim statements to rape counselors. Seven states, three of which are in the preceding group of twelve, have enacted legislation which gives some confidentiality to statements made by victims of domestic violence to staff members at domestic violence shelters.

There are very few statements the law considers confidential. The law does not usually permit people to hold secrets that might be of value to a judge or jury trying to resolve a dispute. The attorney-client privilege is perhaps the best known confidentiality principle. Essentially, this privilege—which has existed since at least the reign of Elizabeth I—protects a client seeking legal advice from a lawyer. Over forty states protect such communications by statute, and other states have created the privilege by court rule or decision.

The marital privilege protects confidential communications made between a husband and a wife during their marriage. Forty-seven states have enacted legislation to protect such communications, although in most states the privilege does not apply in legal actions by one spouse against the other or in child abuse cases. The physician-patient privilege protects communications necessary to enable a physician to treat a patient. The clergyman-penitent privilege protects communications made during a confessional relationship.

Privileges for communications between rape counselors and victims is part of a broader movement to protect communications between mental health professionals and their patients. For instance, six states have created a psychiatrist-patient privilege, and ten states have a social worker–client privilege.

Of the twelve states that have established a sexual assault counselor–victim privilege, all but two protect all confidential communications, typically defined as information exchanged between a victim and a counselor, in confidence, and in circumstances where the victim is assured communications will not be disclosed to a third person. Child abuse counselors are sometimes exempted from the privilege, however. In some states the privilege includes communications between the counselor and the victim's family and friends, but in most states the privilege applies only to the victim.

Confidentiality can be waived of course by the victim, and in three states, a judge may privately examine the records of rape counselors–victim statements and then order the counselor to testify concerning those communications.

Almost all states have a specific definition of a rape counselor, usually a person who renders services through a victim assistance organization, who is supervised in some way, and who has received some amount of specialized training—forty hours is the typical minimum. In a few states, the type of training is described, whether it is medical, legal, and so on.

If you are a victim of sexual assault, it is important to know whether your state has a privilege for communications between you and rape counselors. The law changes quickly in this field, but the states that as of the publication of this book have such a privilege in some form are California, Connecticut, Florida, Illinois, Maine, Minnesota, New Jersey, New York, Ohio, Pennsylvania, Washington, and Wisconsin. Legislation to create such a privilege has been introduced in twenty other states. A local rape counselor will know whether your state has a privilege. Don't be reluctant to ask about it.

In a number of reported cases in states without this privilege, sexual assault counselors have refused—even in the face of a court order—to turn over records that contained notes of confidential communications from victims. Some of these counselors have gone to jail rather than reveal victim confidences. In other reported cases, rape crisis centers have successfully convinced courts that, even in the absence of a statute, victim communications to counselors should remain confidential.

Rape Trauma Syndrome

Rape trauma syndrome is used to describe a collection of symptoms commonly found in rape victims: shock, self-blame, disorientation, nightmares, fear of retaliation, and fear of being raped again. First described in 1972 by rape counselors the syndrome originally was designed as a therapeutic tool for physicians and rape counselors. In recent years, prosecutors have attempted to use evidence of rape trauma syndrome to prove that the victim was, in fact, sexually assaulted.

The courts have viewed such evidence, however, with disfavor for two reasons. First, some courts have questioned whether there is sufficient scientific data to support the existence of rape trauma syndrome. Second, and perhaps more reasonably, some courts have accepted the validity of rape trauma syndrome but argue that evidence of it does not prove or even tend to prove the defendant charged with the crime is the individual who committed the sexual assault, only that a sexual assault took place.

The Minnesota Supreme Court reversed the conviction of a man convicted of rape following the introduction at his trial of evidence that the victim suffered from rape trauma syndrome. Courts in Kansas, Oregon, Missouri, and Montana have refused to allow testimony of rape trauma syndrome. The Supreme Court of California expressed skepticism about the existence of the syndrome. The court also speculated whether defense attorneys should be entitled to have their own psychiatrist examine the victim of a sexual assault where the prosecution intended to introduce evidence of rape trauma syndrome.

Courts will continue to examine the scientific validity of the syndrome, and wrestle with the fairness of introducing evidence about it.

If you become a rape victim or the victim of any other sexual assault, get immediate medical attention—not because of any legal requirement, but because it is a matter of health. If the crime has not been reported to the police, consider whether you want to do so. You may want to discuss the question of whether to report a rape with your rape counselor. Because of the emotional trauma experienced by many sexual assault victims, you should recognize that recovery from such an assault is not synonymous with a return to good physical health. Don't be afraid to ask for mental health counseling if you need it. Self-treatment may be appropriate for some, but it is not for everyone.

RAPE CRISIS CENTERS

Rape Response Program
Birmingham, AL
(205) 323-7273

Council Against Rape/
Lighthouse
Montgomery, AL
(205) 263-4481

Standing Together Against
Rape
Anchorage, AK
(907) 276-7273

Center Against Sexual Assault
Phoenix, AZ
(602) 279-9824

Tucson Rape Crisis Center, Inc.
Tucson, AZ
(602) 624-7273

Rape Crisis, Inc.
Little Rock, AR
(501) 375-1395

Sexual Assault Crisis Center
Los Angeles, CA
(213) 295-8582

San Francisco Women Against
Rape
San Francisco, CA
(415) 647-7273

Rape Crisis Service
Boulder, CO
(303) 443-7300

Sexual Assault Crisis Services
Hartford, CT
(203) 525-1163

Rape Crisis Center
Wilmington, DE
(302) 658-5011

D.C. Rape Crisis Center
Washington DC
(202) 333-7273

Rape Treatment Center
Miami, FL
(305) 325-6941

Rape Crisis Center
Atlanta, GA
(404) 588-4861

Sexual Abuse Treatment Center
Honolulu, HI
(808) 947-8337

YWCA Women's Crisis Center
Boise, ID
(208) 343-3688

Coalition Against Sexual
Assault
Springfield, IL
(217) 753-4117

Women United Against Rape
P.O. Box 2617
Gary, IN
(219) 937-0450

Coalition Against Sexual Abuse
1158 27th St.
Des Moines, IA
(515) 271-2918

Wichita Area Rape Center
Wichita, KS
(316) 263-0185

R.A.P.E. Relief Center
Louisville, KY
(502) 581-7273

YWCA Rape Crisis Service
New Orleans, LA
(504) 488-2693

Rape Crisis Center
Portland, ME
(207) 774-3613

Baltimore Center for Victims of
Sexual Assault
Baltimore, MD
(301) 366-7273

Boston Area Rape Crisis Center
Cambridge, MA
(617) 492-7273

Rape Counseling Center
Detroit, MI
(313) 832-2530

Victims of Sexual Assault
St. Paul, MN
(612) 296-7084

Rape Crisis Center
Jackson, MS
(601) 355-5520

Sexual Assault Treatment
Center
Kansas City, MO
(816) 932-2171

Rape Awareness Program
Helena, MT
(406) 443-5353

Women Against Violence
Omaha, NE
(402) 345-7273

Community Action Against
Rape
Las Vegas, NV
(702) 735-1111

Women's Crisis Line
Manchester, NH
(603) 625-5785

Sexual Assault Rape Analysis
Unit
Newark, NJ
(201) 733-7273

Albuquerque Rape Crisis
Center
Albuquerque, NM
(505) 247-0707

Rape Crisis Program
New York, NY
(212) 790-8068

Rape Crisis Center
Syracuse, NY
(315) 422-7273

Charlotte-Mecklenburg Rape
Crisis Service
Charlotte, NC
(704) 373-0982

Rape and Abuse Crisis Center
Fargo, ND
(701) 293-7273

Women Helping Women
Cincinnati, OH
(513) 381-6003

Women Against Rape
Columbus, OH
(614) 221-4447

Call Rape
Tulsa, OK
(918) 742-7620

Rape Victim Advocate Project
Portland, OR
(503) 248-5059

Women Organized Against
Rape
Philadelphia, PA
(215) 922-7400

Pittsburgh Action Against Rape
Pittsburgh, PA
(412) 682-0219

Centro De Ayuda a Victimas de
Violacion
Caparra Heights, PR
(809) 765-2285

Rhode Island Rape Crisis
Center
Providence, RI
(401) 941-2400

People Against Rape
Charleston, SC
(803) 722-7273

Aberdeen Area Rape Task Force
Aberdeen, SD
(605) 226-1212

Comprehensive Rape Crisis
Program
Memphis, TN
(901) 528-2161

Dallas County Rape Crisis
Center
Dallas, TX
(214) 521-1020

Rape Crisis Center
Houston, TX
(713) 528-6798

Rape Crisis Center
West Valley City, UT
(801) 532-7273

Women's Rape Crisis Center
Burlington, VT
(802) 863-1236

Rape Crisis Group
Charlottesville, VA
(804) 295-7273

Seattle Rape Relief
Seattle, WA
(206) 226-5062

Sexual Assault Information
Center
Charleston, WV
(304) 344-9839

Wisconsin Coalition Against
Sexual Assault
Madison, WI
(608) 251-5457

Safe House/Sexual Assault
Services
Cheyenne, WY 82003
(307) 634-8655

·7·

Compensation, Restitution, and Taxes

Financial benefits to crime victims are mandated by law in some states but vary from state to state. Generally, there are two types of such benefits, compensation and restitution. Compensation refers to money paid by the state to the crime victim, a person or organization that assisted the victim, or, in the case of murder, to the victim's survivors. Restitution, which is usually ordered by the court, refers to money paid by the convicted offender to the victim.

Under the laws establishing victim compensation programs, some victims can receive funds from the state to help pay costs associated with being a victim—medical or psychiatric expenses, wages lost, and so forth. Compensation for victims of crime is not a right, however, and unless your state or the state in which you become a victim (if nonresidents are compensated) has a compensation program, you cannot receive funds. Forty states, the District of Columbia, and Puerto Rico have these programs.

Although these programs have existed since 1966, very

few crime victims know of them, and many of those who are eligible fail to apply. A survey in New Jersey, a state that has had a compensation program for over a decade, found that fewer than five percent of all eligible victims applied for compensation. One reason so few victims know of the programs is that they receive very little publicity. A few states require the police to notify all crime victims about the existence of such a program, and program directors do try to publicize their availability, but most crime victims are unaware they can apply for benefits.

How to Apply for Victim Compensation

To see if your state has a program, call the victim/witness assistance unit in your state, listed at the end of Chapter 1. The people there will also give you the name of the victim compensation agency and tell you how to contact it.

To be eligible for an award, you must report the crime to the police or appropriate law enforcement agency. You cannot be compensated for injuries associated with unreported crimes. In addition, you will have a continuing duty to cooperate with the police and other law enforcement officials, including the prosecutors. Eligible victims can be denied compensation because they fail to cooperate with law enforcement officials.

Second, you may need an attorney to assist you in making your claim. In a number of states, victim compensation awards are administered by the court of claims, which means it is almost essential to have an attorney. In other states, the process is complicated enough so that an attorney will be of great assistance to you, and may even be essential. (See Chapter 2 for methods of obtaining an attorney.)

In some states an attorney will cost you nothing, because the compensation statute provides for attorneys' fees as a separate award (up to a specified amount). In other states, attorneys' fees are subtracted from the award paid to the victim. You may wish to consult the staff of the victim/witness assistance unit to ask whether you need an attorney to file a compensation claim.

Whether or not you employ an attorney, remember that after a compensation claim is filed, you will probably receive a questionnaire from the victim compensation agency. The agency will use your answers as a first step to determine eligiblity so be careful how you answer. If you intend to use an attorney, employ him or her before you answer questions from the state agency. If you do not use an attorney, study the questionnaire very carefully, and take your time answering it. An inaccurate answer could result in your being denied an award.

From the moment you suffer injury, keep complete and accurate records of your costs. Do not concern yourself with whether or not you'll be compensated for a loss, keep the records and worry later about which records you will need. If some of your losses or costs are reimbursed by an insurance company or a government agency other than the victim compensation program (such as Medicare, Medicaid, Veterans Administration, etc.), be sure to keep copies of the reimbursement vouchers. You may have to establish at some future time how much you received and from whom. If you miss work, be sure your employer knows you are absent because you were a victim. If you are eligible to receive compensation for lost wages, you will have to prove how much of your absence from work was attributable to injuries you suffered as a result of the crime.

Expect some delays even if you are awarded compensation. Some state victim compensation agencies process claims very quickly, but others do not. In one state, it takes over two years for the eligible victims to learn they will receive awards, followed by further delay before payment is actually made. In some states, the agency may have insufficient funds to pay claims because the funding source—fines paid to the court or some other form of revenue—lacks enough money to pay all eligible compensation claims. When that happens, the states make awards in the order in which the claims were filed.

Some states have emergency awards. If you or someone you know is a victim without funds, the victim compensation agency may be able to make an emergency award even before all of the formal paperwork has been completed. Call your state agency to ask about this.

Almost without exception, if you are denied compensation, you are entitled to an explanation why, and you may even be entitled to a hearing with respect to your claim. Whether you demand such a hearing is a question you should discuss with a victim counselor (if one is available) or an attorney. Then the decision by the state agency to deny you an award can be reviewed by the state courts. Again, you should discuss your claim with someone familiar with the applicable state statute before you consider suing the victim compensation agency.

Eligibility

Not every crime victim is eligible for compensation. All states have restrictions and limitations. Most programs do not award benefits if the person who commits the crime is related by blood or marriage to the victim seeking benefits. These and other programs also deny benefits to victims injured by a person living in the same home with the victim whether or not they are related. Victims most frequently affected by these eligibility limitations include children who are physically or sexually abused by their parents or other relatives, those abused by a spouse, and elderly people abused by those who are supposed to be caring for them.

The related-to-the-victim limitation rules were passed to prevent the perpetrator from benefiting from the criminal act. For instance, if a father physically abuses his children, who then need medical or psychiatric attention, why should the state pay for these services when the father is the one who should pay for the needs of his children? While this argument might seem to make sense, it suffers from several fatal flaws. First, it assumes the father (or any other relative responsible for a crime victim's injuries) has the financial resources to pay for the services his children need, something that is not always true. Second, it assumes that if the father has such financial resources, he will use them to care for the children he abused. If he is a fugitive, the state may not even be able to find the father, much less be able to force him to pay.

This limitation of eligibility adds to another problem. Typically, in child abuse and spouse abuse cases, the victim is financially dependent on the person responsible for the crime and will decline to prosecute and may not even report the crime. To force the victim to rely on the perpetrator to pay for the injuries suffered is completely unreasonable.

This limitation on family member benefits has led to some outrageous decisions. For instance, one court denied compensation to the child of a woman stabbed to death by a man who had earlier raped her. The child was conceived as a result of this sexual assault, in fact. The court reasoned that even though no legal family relationship existed between the man and the child under the applicable state law, the father and child were "family" within the meaning of the compensation act. In another case, a homicide victim's family was denied compensation because one of the two perpetrators of the crime was related to the survivors. In yet another case, children who survived the murder of their mother were denied compensation because the convicted murderer was their father.

A number of states deny compensation awards to non-resident crime victims, and most states compensate resident crime victims only when the crime was committed within the state. In a few instances, states permit compensation awards to nonresident crime victims if the victim is a resident of a state that permits nonresidents to receive compensation awards.

Crime victim compensation statutes almost always require the person compensated to be an "innocent victim" of crime. That rule has led to the denial of awards in cases in which the victim was injured in a fight with the perpetrator, but investigation revealed it was the "victim" who started the fight. While that rule has obvious merit, it has been expanded in some states to require the victim to "back down" when confronted by the perpetrator, which implies that if you are confronted by a person who wants to fight, you have a duty to retreat. If you fail to retreat—if you stand your ground—you are not an innocent victim of an assault. (See Chapter 8 for a discussion of self-defense.)

Of course, innocent victim is a legal description subject to varying interpretations. We can define "victim" but the word "innocent" causes problems. For instance, in a Midwestern state, a young woman assaulted in a bar was denied compensation, after police reports showed she had been arrested in the past on prostitution charges. Although she was not working as a prostitute when assaulted, she was not "innocent" in the eyes of the victim compensation board because of her criminal record.

Almost without exception, victim compensation statutes deny awards to victims of automobile accidents on the grounds that they are not "crime" victims, even if the other driver is intoxicated or driving without a license. Nor is compensation awarded if the driver flees after his car strikes the victim to be arrested later. Essentially, victim compensation statutes require that the perpetrator of the incident intended to harm the victim. If the perpetrator is simply negligent—even grossly negligent so that his conduct could result in his being charged with a crime—the victim is ineligible for an award because the perpetrator's conduct was unintentional. A few compensation boards and courts have permitted awards where the perpetrator committed a criminal act not directly involving the victim but struck the victim with a vehicle while fleeing the scene of the crime.

Other eligibility limitations decrease the number of victims who receive awards, the most important of which is the collateral source rule, which reduces compensation to the extent the victim has been compensated by others. For instance, if you suffer physical injuries that require both hospitalization and a doctor's care, you will not receive benefits for the medical expenses paid for by an insurance policy. You cannot recover twice from two different sources.

In addition, some states have a financial hardship test that limits compensation to crime victims who are without financial resources or who have very few financial resources and denies compensation to those who are capable of paying for the costs of caring for their injuries themselves.

Benefits

All states with victim compensation programs provide specific benefits and compensation for certain losses but also restrict benefits in a number of different ways. Without exception, a crime victim cannot receive compensation for stolen property for several reasons. First, fraud might be prevalent in some claims. While medical services, burial expenses, lost wages or even job retraining are crime victim expenses that can be established, the value of property allegedly stolen, or even the existence of such property, is very difficult to verify.

Second, property theft and damage as a result of criminal activity costs billions of dollars a year. The cost of arson exceeds $200 million a year, and that is only one property crime, albeit a serious one. In the last fiscal year for which statistics are available, 1982, the total victim compensation paid by all states was less than $50 million. Obviously if property theft were compensated for, the cost of victim compensation programs would be dramatically higher.

Costs that can be compensated for typically include: funeral and burial costs; hospital costs; and physicians' and other health care providers' fees. In most states, such costs are paid directly to the provider of the service. Very few programs provide for pain and suffering awards.

Restitution

Restitution can provide direct monetary awards to victims, as the person convicted of a crime must pay the victim for the purpose of making the victim whole, or putting the victim in the same position as before the crime. Restitution—in some states referred to as reparation—can take many forms, both of money and services.

Of course, before determining how much restitution the victim is entitled to, the judge must have some information about what happened to the victim as a result of the crime. That information is not always available. Approximately 90 percent of all criminal cases are resolved through pleas of guilty by the defendant (usually to a crime less serious than the one charged), and thus trial judges rarely see the victim, let alone learn about their economic losses. Even when a case proceeds to trial, the victims' testimony may focus only on the events of the crime without any mention of physical injuries or economic losses. In some states, victim impact statements provide this.

For many years, defendants convicted of felonies in every state were given a presentence report, which described the defendants' prior criminal record if any, family background, education, work experience, and likelihood of work opportunities in the future. But what about the victim? Until recently, judges were not very concerned about the victims and rarely if ever inquired about the effects of the crime on them. In fact, most judges were of the view—some still are—that victims of crime had no place in the sentencing process.

Victim impact statements are beginning to change this, although in some states victims remain absent from the sentencing process. Victim impact statements are sometimes required by statute—such as in Maryland and Ohio—and provide detailed information to be given to the judge, which include identification of the victims, a list of the economic losses suffered, information about any physical or emotional injury incurred, and a description of any change in the personal welfare or family relations of the victim. In some states, even if no presentence report is ordered, a victim impact statement may be prepared.

In some states, the victim's loss of earnings is specifically included in the statement, while in others an inquiry is made into the effect the crime has had on immediate family members of the victim. In Illinois and Minnesota, the victim is permitted to recommend a sentence, and in a few states the victim can object to the sentence imposed. Many victim impact statements permit victims to state whether they believe they face a threat of harm if the defendant is not sent to prison.

Although a judge can permit a victim to address the court at sentencing, some states—including Connecticut and Arizona—have enacted legislation to permit the practice in all cases. The victim, members of the victim's family, or the victim's lawyer may appear before the court before or at sentencing to tell the judge what sentence they feel should be imposed.

It is impossible to describe all available sentences a judge can impose, but in its simplest form, sentencing can be divided into several categories. The sentence can send the defendant to prison for a specific term (i.e., five years), or for a term of years (i.e., not less than three or more than nine years), or for an indeterminate term with the defendant's release date determined by the parole board. A sentence of probation does not send the defendant to prison; the defendant remains free, but on probation for a period of time—usually five or fewer years. Probation allows the defendant to remain at liberty as long as certain conditions are met, usually no further convictions. Certain other conditions also apply, such as remaining employed, being home no later than a particular time, reporting to the probation officer at specified times, and perhaps paying restitution to the victim of the crime.

The majority of restitution orders are imposed on defendants who are sentenced to probation. However, in New York and several other states, restitution can be imposed on a defendant who is sentenced to prison. In these cases, the funds the victim receives from the defendant are based on the defendant's earnings while in prison, or after release from prison, while on parole.

The Amount of Restitution

There are several problems associated with restitution, but among the most difficult is the question of how much is appropriate. If the defendant stole $100 from the victim, who then lost $50 in wages while cooperating with the authorities in the arrest and prosecution, the amount of restitution—$150—is relatively easy to determine. But what about the case where the victim lost no money but suffered permanent injury as the result of an assault? How much restitution is appropriate? In some states, when a defendant is guilty of a violent crime injuring the victim, restitution may not be imposed if the amount is in dispute or is not easily discernible, although in a few other states restitution can be ordered in this situation. Of course, if the defendant agrees to the amount of restitution, there will be no dispute about the amount being appropriate. For instance, in one assault case a restitution order of $12,000 was upheld because the defendant agreed to that amount, even though it was unclear whether the $12,000 was for medical expenses, lost wages, or something else.

Restitution is generally not limited by the amount of a fine the defendant must pay as a result of the conviction. Thus, if a person is sentenced to probation and also ordered to pay a fine of $1,000, he still could be ordered to pay the victim $5,000. If a victim sues a defendant who has previously been ordered to pay restitution and wins, the amount of damages awarded to the victim will be reduced by the amount of the restitution.

Restitution can be ordered for a victim's medical expenses, including hospital and physician costs, lost wages, funeral expenses, damage to property, and practically any other expense or lost income a victim may have suffered. In the majority of states, courts have held it is also permissible to order a defendant to pay the victim for the "pain and suffering" the victim experienced.

In some cases, courts have ordered restitution to persons other than the direct victim of the crime. For example, in murder cases courts have ordered restitution payments to be made to the family of the victim. In a number of cases, courts have ordered defendants to pay restitution to insurance companies to reimburse them for the medical insurance payments they made to the victim. Employers have received restitution payments for the loss of services of their employee, the victim.

Restitution has also been ordered for some offenses not traditionally thought of as serious crimes, such as driving while intoxicated, reckless driving, and disorderly conduct.

Limitations on Restitution

In most states, restitution is ordered as a condition of probation. If the defendant fails to follow the conditions of probation—including making restitution payments—the defendant can be sent to prison.

But what if the defendant is unable to make restitution through no fault of his own? Suppose the defendant is unemployable, or is employed but later loses his job? If the defendant is imprisoned because he is unable to make restitution, he is sent to prison for debt—one of the conditions that led the early colonists to leave England for this country.

Most courts have held that failure to make restitution can lead to imprisonment, not for debt but rather for violation of the probation. However, the courts have also stated that indefinite restitution—requiring a person to pay restitution for the rest of his life—is constitutionally impermissible because it reduces the defendant to a state of peonage. Thus restitution must be for a specific amount and cannot be ordered as a "life sentence."

In 1982 Congress passed the Victim and Witness Protection Act, which authorizes restitution to victims by people convicted of federal crimes. Restitution is not a substitute for victim compensation. While most crimes have victims, very few crimes have defendants who are arrested, convicted (or plead guilty), and are thereafter in a position to make restitution. In fact people have criticized restitution because it favors the wealthy defendant. Judges are far quicker to sentence a wealthy defendant to probation and to order restitution as a condition of that probation than to sentence a poor person to probation and restitution because judges assume the poor defendant will be unable to pay restitution. But for the most part restitution is underutilized, and only a few states require a judge to consider restitution. One reason many judges are reluctant to order restitution is their perception that most convicted felons are unable to make restitution. Nobody knows for sure if this is true, but several years ago, in North Carolina, a state that does not have a victim compensation program, over $3 million in restitution was collected during one year. Either North Carolina has the richest group of convicted felons in the country—which is highly unlikely—or else a restitution program is effective when people are willing to consider it.

If you are a victim, remember that your involvement in the criminal justice process does not end with the conviction or guilty plea of the defendant; you should be involved in the sentencing process. If you are in a state where victim impact statements are not routinely used, file your own victim impact statement in the absence of someone else filing one: write to the judge who will impose sentence and describe what happened to you as a result of the crime. You should explain what financial losses you had to give the sentencing judge some measure of damages in the event restitution is considered.

Finally, if you want to watch the sentencing of the defendant or be heard at the sentencing, you should attend. Some judges will not permit you to participate actively in sentencing, but as more and more victims demand that right, the courts will be forced to recognize that victims have rights—even after the defendant's conviction.

Tax and Insurance Issues
Affecting Victims of Crime

The economic losses some victims experience may be tax deductible, may be covered by the victim's insurance, or may be compensated through the insurance of the perpetrator or a third party. Sometimes indirect losses, such as lost wages, can also be compensated through insurance.

With respect to taxes, the victim absolutely must consult his or her own accountant or lawyer before claiming deductions as the result of a crime. The deductibility of losses varies from taxpayer to taxpayer, and sometimes from state to state. Only very general principles can be described here, and some of those are applicable to different victims in different ways and in different amounts.

First, losses unsubstantiated by records and documents can be deducted only at the peril of the taxpayer. The Internal Revenue Service will not take your word for the fact that you suffered a loss as the result of a crime; you must be able to prove it. For some taxpayers, written records are the only acceptable proof. Therefore, keep all records of your loss: police reports, expenses for the replacement value of lost or stolen property, medical bills, etc. Except for small losses, under $100, you may deduct the value of your loss, but without written records to support them, your deductions will not be allowed, and your inability to prove the losses after claiming them may result in your having to pay interest or even a penalty tax.

For some taxpayers, the value of cash or lost or stolen property not compensated by insurance may be deducted from gross income reported on the federal tax return if the taxpayer itemized deductions. In states with income tax, such loss may be deducted from gross income on the state income tax return. Thus if property is stolen from you during the commission of a burglary or robbery, under some conditions the losses are deductible. Generally, the government permits deductions as the result of a loss only to the amount of the present value of the item lost, not the replacement value.

If you don't report the crime to the police, the tax authorities will probably disallow any loss claimed. Similarly, the extent of your loss as described in a police report may not be less than the amount claimed on your tax return. Some tax authorities may require you to prove the value of the stolen item by the receipt you received when you purchased it, if that is how you acquired it. As noted below, some insurance companies have the same requirements for losses claimed under an insurance policy.

If a victim pays for medical services and receives no compensation through insurance, a victim compensation program, or a restitution order for such payments, the advice of a professional tax preparer will probably be necessary to determine the amount of the deduction. As with other types of losses, however, a professional tax consultant will be unable to help the victim without records supporting the amount of the medical deductions claimed.

There are other deductions certain taxpayers may be able to claim, and an accountant or lawyer should be consulted about the amount and the extent of such deductions.

Insurance policies may compensate crime victims in a number of ways. First, many so-called homeowners' policies or renters' policies will compensate victims for property stolen from the apartment or house. In addition, many such policies provide limited coverage for losses that occur outside the house or apartment, such as property stolen from a hotel room or a car.

Some victims have health insurance that compensates them for medical expenses although some policies limit the amount of psychiatric or psychological medical expenses that are insured. The insurance can be maintained through an employer's group policy or on an individual basis.

As with tax deductions, insurance claims inevitably require presenting precise records before a claim will be paid, so victims must be prepared to document their losses.

Recently, some victims have tried to make claims against the offenders' homeowners insurance by arguing that their insurance covered any claim for bodily injury occurring on the policyholder's premises. If the victim was injured in the offender's home, it was argued, why shouldn't the victim be indemnified by the insurance company that covered the homeowner?

Almost without exception, insurance policies exclude deliberate acts from coverage; homeowners' policies are intended to insure only acts of negligence. Insuring deliberate acts would be against public policy because monetary fines would lose any deterrent value if paid by an insurance company. However, victims have argued that sexual abuse of children and adults committed by defendants in their homes did not fall within the deliberate act exclusion because the policyholders did not intend to cause physical or psychological injury. This is an important issue in many cases because the offender may not have sufficient funds to pay for the victim's injuries, but the offender's insurance company will have sufficient funds.

Thus far, in the two states where this issue has been presented to the courts, Minnesota and Arkansas, the victims' position has been rejected on the grounds that as a matter of law the offender's conduct could be inferred to involve the intentional infliction of harm.

If you are a crime victim, find out from the police or the prosecutor whether or not your state has a compensation program. If it does, determine whether you are eligible for compensation. If it doesn't, but the person who victimized you has been caught, ask the prosecutor about restitution.

For compensation, restitution, and tax and insurance purposes, document your losses by keeping accurate records of your expenses or lost wages and income.

If the offender is convicted or pleads guilty, ask about a victim impact statement and about your right to be present at sentencing. Tell the sentencing judge through a statement or in person what the effect of the crime was on you. Describe any physical or emotional pain as well as economic losses such as wages you were not paid because you were a victim. If you believe the offender should go to prison, say so.

Your rights as a crime victim must be exercised by you. They are not transferrable to anyone else.

·8·

Self-Defense

While walking down the street near your home, you hear a sound and you turn to see two young men running toward you, one of whom you think is holding a knife. They approach you, and the one with the knife says, "Do you have a wallet?" At this point, is it legally permissible to hit or throw something at one or both of them? If you were in a state that permitted you to carry a gun, could you draw the weapon and order the young men to go away? Could you shoot them? Suppose you're carrying Mace or some other self-protection device; can you pull it out and shoot it in their direction?

Suppose you're in bed in your home late at night when you're awakened by a noise from another room; you get out of bed and walk into the other room where a man is climbing through the window. Can you shoot him? Are you required to ask him to identify himself and explain why he is climbing through the window?

Perhaps the ultimate right of a crime victim is the right not to become a victim at all. When you consider that almost everyone at some time in his or her life will become the victim of a crime, it is important to know what legal rights a person has when confronted by a criminal act. To what extent does the law permit you to protect your property, your loved ones, and yourself?

Some self-defense legal issues are complicated, and, as with other legal principles, the states have different rules. The various standards are described below. At the outset, however, it is important to remember that in self-defense, a mistake or a misunderstanding of what was happening can cause an innocent person to be hurt or killed, and another person—who never intended to harm anyone—to be arrested and charged with assault or murder.

For instance, suppose you shoot and kill the person climbing through the window, who turns out not to be a burglar or a rapist but your next-door neighbor who, because he was slightly intoxicated, was unable to find his house key and was climbing through the window of what he believed was his home. Suppose the two young men who run up and ask you if you have a wallet, saw you drop the wallet and want to bring it to your attention.

Self-defense is a legal principle stating that you may use reasonable force to protect yourself or your property or another person from an adversary whom you reasonably believe is going to harm you or them. The amount of force you may use to protect your property is usually less than the amount you may use to protect yourself, and where you are when you use force may determine the sort of force you may use.

The Amount of Reasonable Force

The law of self-defense recognizes two types of force, deadly and nondeadly. Deadly force is that used with the intent to kill or seriously harm someone, or that which creates a substantial risk of this happening. Nondeadly force is any force less than deadly force.

With certain limitations, you may use deadly force against another person if you reasonably believe that he or she is about to kill or seriously harm you *and* that you must use deadly force to protect yourself. Nondeadly force may be used for the same reasons when faced with a lesser threat. What constitutes a "reasonable belief" will be described below.

There are some additional requirements before you can use force in self-defense. First, the threat must be imminent; if someone threatens to hurt or even kill you tomorrow, or next week, you may not draw your weapon and shoot him today. If the threatened violence is conditional ("If I see you in this neighborhood again, I'll kill you.") or is set in the future, neither deadly nor nondeadly force may be used at the time of the threat. Of course, if and when the threatener does try to attack you, you may be permitted to use some force in self-defense.

Second, while there is no duty to retreat before using nondeadly force, even if you could easily and perhaps sensibly do so, under some circumstances in some states there is a duty to retreat before using deadly force in self-defense. The law about the duty to retreat is not the same or even similar in every state, but some general principles are important: you do not have to retreat if doing so increases the danger to you.

If you are in danger because the person threatening you is attempting or committing another crime—other than assaulting you—you do not have to retreat before using deadly force. If your assailant retreats, however, removing you from imminent danger, you may not use force.

Almost without exception, if you are attacked inside your home, there is no duty to retreat. You may use deadly force in self-defense if it is necessary to save your own life, the life of another, or to prevent serious injury. One exception is that in some states, if you are attacked by a guest, a person who lives with you, or anyone who is lawfully inside your house, you must retreat before using deadly force.

The states are about evenly divided on your duty to retreat outside your home before using deadly force; some require you to retreat first but others do not. To the extent that there is a trend in this area, it appears that more states are adopting a duty-to-retreat standard.

Recently, a New York City resident shot four young men on a subway when they allegedly approached him and demanded money, a case that has received widespread publicity. While this case remains before the courts and the facts have not been fully presented, certain issues are not in dispute. First, the man who did the shooting, Bernhard Goetz, carried a loaded pistol into the subway, which is a felony in New York. Laws that prohibit the possession of certain weapons do not excuse the person who happened to become the victim of a crime while carrying the prohibited weapon. Second, the use of deadly force, such as a gun, requires some prudence. While it appears Goetz did not injure any innocent party—something of a miracle when you consider he fired many shots in a populated subway car—if he had he might have been civilly liable for the injury. Finally, Goetz apparently made no attempt to retreat, which the law sometimes requires, particularly before the use of deadly force.

Although a few courts have ruled to the contrary, the majority hold that your place of business is like your home in that you have little or no duty to retreat before using deadly force. Of course, in a place of business, there is a greater likelihood of being attacked by a person not technically an intruder—someone there to conduct business—than there is in the home. However, a person who enters the business for the sole purpose of committing a crime is an intruder, not a guest or a person permitted to enter. Therefore, deadly force may be used to resist an attack by such a person.

What Constitutes "Reasonable Belief"

As noted above, before using either deadly or nondeadly force in self-defense, you must have a reasonable belief that you or someone else is in imminent danger of some harm. What constitutes a "reasonable belief"?

Essentially the reasonable belief analysis is as follows: given what the person claiming self-defense saw and all of the surrounding circumstances such as the size of the self-defender versus the size of the attacker, the time of day, the place, whether there was a weapon, and so forth, would a reasonable person have believed there was imminent danger of harm. The question of reasonableness does not turn on necessity or even mistake of fact. It makes no difference whether, in retrospect, the use of a particular act of self-defense was necessary. Rather, the question is whether the person claiming self-defense, under the circumstances as they appeared at the time of the incident, was justified in believing that force was necessary.

If it turns out a person was mistaken about the facts, and the use of force was unneeded, the claim of self-defense does not necessarily fail. Rather, the question is if the mistake was a reasonable one. For instance, if someone approaches and says, "I'm going to shoot you dead," then reaches into a pocket and begins to pull out what appears to you to be a gun, you can use force—even deadly force—to resist. If it turns out the gun was only a water pistol, your use of deadly force would still be based on a reasonable belief, albeit a mistaken one. On the other hand, if you knew this person was a practical joker who carried a water pistol with which he pretended to threaten people, your decision to use deadly force—or perhaps any force—would not be based on a reasonable belief.

A famous Supreme Court justice put it best when he noted that "detached reflection cannot be demanded in the presence of an uplifted knife." But you must believe it is a real knife and not the rubber knife used by a practical joker.

There are limits on how mistaken one can be. For instance, a person who voluntarily becomes high on drugs or intoxicated on liquor and cannot think clearly enough to form a reasonable belief will be hard put to claim self-defense if a sober person would not have made the same mistake of fact.

Finally, what if a person uses force unreasonably against what appears to be an aggressor? If the person claiming self-defense negligently used deadly force, and mistakenly and unreasonably killed someone else, how does the law treat the act? In most jurisdictions it is not murder. Instead, the courts have adopted what is called the "imperfect self-defense doctrine," which states that while not innocent of any crime, the actor is not guilty of murder but of a lesser crime, perhaps manslaughter or negligent homicide.

Defense of Other People

Under some circumstances you can use force to defend another person, although there are more limitations than if you were defending yourself. In most states all three of the following conditions must be met to use force in someone else's defense.

First, you must reasonably believe that this person would be justified in using the same amount of force to protect himself which you are using instead. For instance, you may not use deadly force if he or she would be justified in using only nondeadly force. If he or she would not use any force, neither may you. Simply stated, you stand in the shoes of the person you seek to protect in determining whether force can be used, and, if so, how much.

Second, you must reasonably believe the other person is in imminent danger of death or injury, and again, you stand in his or her shoes. There is the possibility, however, that you, as the rescuer, might have greater reason to use force than would the victim. For instance, suppose you saw what you believed was a robbery by a perpetrator who appeared to be unarmed. In the victim's place you might be prohibited from using deadly force. But suppose you knew this robber always killed his victims with a gun hidden in his pocket after getting the money. Under those circumstances, your increased awareness of the real danger to the victim might make your use of force, even deadly force, a reasonable act.

Third, you must believe your intervention is necessary to protect the victim. If the victim is retreating or does not appear to be in danger or has someone else coming to his or her rescue making your intervention unnecessary, you may not use force to protect the victim.

All three of these conditions must be present before you may use force to protect another person.

Special Circumstances

Accidental injury to a third person. If you are in a situation where you may properly use deadly or nondeadly force in self-defense, and in doing so kill or injure an innocent person, what is your criminal liability? If force was properly used, you are not held responsible by criminal law for the death or injury of a third person. Take the following example, which is based on an actual case: X is assaulted by Y and reasonably believes he must use deadly force to protect himself by firing a gun. Y ducks, and the bullet strikes Z, an innocent bystander, who is killed. If the use of deadly force by X was reasonable, as a matter of criminal law, X is not liable for the death of Z. However, it certainly would not be reasonable for X to deliberately kill Z in order to get a better shot at Y. X is permitted to defend himself, but not by killing or wounding every innocent person in his line of fire. If X kills Z in order to get a better shot at Y, Z's heirs could sue both X and Y for the death of Z.

Resisting lawful/unlawful arrest. In some states, you may use nondeadly force to resist an unlawful arrest, which happens if the police have neither probable cause to believe you committed a crime nor a warrant for your arrest. In such a case, the threatened harm to you is not death or injury, but indignity, humiliation, and illegal detention that accompany the arrest. In other states, however, you are forbidden to use force of any kind to resist an arrest.

But suppose you see what appears to be a fight with X and Y beating Z. You decide to come to Z's rescue and enter the fight to help him resist them. Suppose it turns out that X and Y are plainclothes police officers who are trying lawfully to arrest Z. Have you committed a crime? In some states, you could be arrested for helping Z assault a police officer and unlawfully resisting arrest. In other states, the courts would find you innocent if your belief that Z was the innocent victim of an assault was a reasonable one. In any event, when defending an "innocent victim," you should be sure that the "assailant" is not a police officer.

Excessive force. In the examples above, the force used in self-defense or defense of a third person is a gun or knife. What about more dangerous weapons such as a shotgun or even a machine gun? Under federal law, you may not possess a machine gun for any purpose unless you are in the armed forces, nor may you alter a shotgun by sawing off a part of the barrel to make it more dangerous. In addition, the reasonableness standards described above also apply to the amount of deadly or nondeadly force you use. For instance, if you were attacked in your home by an intruder, the use of a shotgun would almost certainly be permissible. However, if you were attacked in a crowded room and fired a shotgun, striking the attacker as well as five innocent people, the authorities would question whether you had used too much force to protect yourself. Even though self-defense is permitted, you may not endanger people in your line of fire, particularly if less force could have been used.

Defense of property where there is no threat to you. If you know an intruder is about to enter or is in your home or place of business and has no intention of harming you but does intend to steal your property, in most states, the use of deadly force is not permitted. Nondeadly force is permitted, but not if a demand that the intruder leave will prevent the robbery. In addition, so-called booby traps that involve deadly force may not ordinarily be used to protect property. In most states, an electrified fence that will kill a person rather than just shock him, or explosives that can be triggered by a trespasser, are not permitted. As a general rule, where protection of property is the sole objective, the only force permitted is that which will successfully prevent any harm to the property.

Risk of civil liability. As noted in Chapter 3, an assault, in addition to being a crime, may also be grounds for the victim to sue. Likewise mistakenly using self-defense force against an innocent person may expose you to a civil suit by that person. In short, civil law presents some risks to the person who improperly uses force in self-defense.

It is impossible to memorize all of the rules associated with the use of self-defense and when you have to defend yourself, there is little time to think, or to ponder which rule you should follow and why. The clearest and most concise way of describing the various rules would be: be reasonable. You may avoid becoming a victim, and you may protect yourself, your loved ones, your property, and—if you wish—strangers. But you must do it reasonably. Vigilante actions and conduct reminiscent of the Lone Ranger are good entertainment in the movies, but in real life, they expose you to criminal or civil liability and can lead to the injury or death of innocent people.

·9·

Organizations and Issues

When you consider how difficult change is in a society as complex as ours, the progress made by victim advocates to achieve rights for crime victims has been nothing short of astonishing. During the last ten years, legislation has been enacted at both the state and federal level to ensure victims of crime a place in the criminal justice system.

In 1975, only ten states had victim compensation statutes, but by 1985, forty states and the District of Columbia had such programs. In 1975, only three states funded their domestic violence services, while the rest were forced to look to private gifts; in 1985, forty-nine states provided some government money for these services. Ten years ago, victim impact statements were only a dream in the minds of some victim advocates but now they exist, and in 1985, thirty-one states had some form of victim participation at sentencing. Many states fund local victim/witness assistance units, which was unheard of only a few years ago. Indeed, a few years ago there were no victim/witness assistance units.

Organizations representing many types of crime victims have worked at the state and local level to introduce legislation requiring the police, prosecutors, courts, and correctional personnel to address the needs of crime victims. Different states have gone about this effort in different ways. California, one of the first to enact victim compensation legislation, was also one of the first states to enact a crime victims' bill of rights. (Twenty-eight states have such a Bill of Rights.) Proposition 8, which appeared on the California ballot in 1982, amended the California constitution to provide rights for victims of crime. It became an election issue after 663,000 voters signed a petition to place it on the ballot, and in a general election, over 56 percent of the voters approved the proposition.

California's bill of rights affects defendants' rights as much as it provides greater rights for crime victims by restricting defendants' rights in specific cases and for certain crimes. In some states, however, the victims' bill of rights has done little or nothing to restrict the defendants' rights, and as a result the American Civil Liberties Union, a group often identified with the defendants' rights, has supported greater rights for crime victims in many states.

At the federal level, important legislation has been enacted that affects the rights of crime victims in federal courts and which serves as a model for those states that wish to alter their existing laws. This federal legislation provides much needed funding for crime victim programs at the local level even though crime remains a local problem. Relatively few criminal cases are tried in federal court, and those that are—narcotics cases, mail fraud, and interstate racketeering—typically do not involve crimes of violence against individual victims. However, the federal government not only has the financial resources to influence crime victim legislation throughout the country, it also commands significant public attention so that federal legislation tends to influence that of state and local governments.

Frequently, federal legislation is the result of a study or fact-finding inquiry into a particular problem. In 1982, President Reagan appointed a Task Force on Victims of Crime that held hearings in five cities and heard testimony from over two hundred witnesses. Sixty of these witnesses were victims of crime; the rest were victim advocates and local and federal law enforcement officials. The task force issued a report containing numerous recommendations calling for the recognition of the rights of victims of crime, as well as for funding victim service organizations. The task force recommended abolition of certain evidentiary principles that tend to benefit the accused.

The first federal law affecting crime victims was passed and signed into law. This act, the Victim and Witness Protection Act of 1982, assisted victims in a number of significant ways. It required victim impact statements in all federal criminal cases as part of the presentence report. It also amended existing federal laws, making it a crime to threaten, intimidate, or retaliate against a victim or witness by permitting the government to seek restraining orders in such cases. The act also established restitution programs for federal criminal cases and required a judge to consider restitution as part of any sentence imposed. The act also required the attorney general to issue guidelines for the fair treatment of victims.

Two years later, the Victims of Crime Act of 1984 was passed to develop the rights of crime victims at the local and federal level. The act established a crime victims' fund, which cannot exceed more than $100 million in any fiscal year, to help victims in three ways: up to 50 percent of the fund is to aid state crime victim compensation programs; up to 5 percent of the fund is used for compensating victims of federal crimes; 45 percent of the money (plus funds left over from the first two purposes) is used to aid local crime victim programs.

The fund is supported by fines collected in federal criminal cases and by new and increased penalty assessments for federal crimes, as well as bail forfeited by people who fail to appear in court. The fund is also supported by revenue confiscated from people charged with or convicted of a federal crime who thereafter sell literary or entertainment rights about that crime.

The fund contains a "sunset" provision that terminates the act on September 30, 1988, unless extended by Congress.

The federal government has also funded research and action programs to implement many of the recommendations of the task force. One such program has been undertaken by the American Bar Association's Victims Committee. With the aid of a federal grant, the committee has prepared model legislation in a number of areas affecting victims' rights, including the rights of victims to appear at parole hearings, and the issue of victim/counselor confidentiality. Other model legislation includes the right of employers to receive certain criminal history information about prospective employees, and victim restitution programs, victim impact statements, and guidelines for when and under what circumstances cases should be continued.

Another federal law passed in 1984 should assist crime victims by providing funds for victim service organizations. This law, the Justice Assistance Act of 1984, established within the U.S. Department of Justice an Office of Justice Programs, which provides staff support to a number of existing Department of Justice offices, including the National Institute of Justice and the Bureau of Justice Statistics. More importantly, the new law creates a block grant program through which states are entitled to receive funds for certain law enforcement services, including programs that provide assistance to crime victims.

In 1984 another presidential task force was established. The Family Violence Task Force held public hearings in six cities and heard testimony from over one thousand victims, criminal justice experts, and researchers about the nature and extent of family violence in the United States. The report of the task force includes sixty-five recommendations, many of which concern the importance of treating family violence as a crime where a criminal statute has been violated. Multidisciplinary responses to family violence were recommended, particularly in cases involving physical and sexual abuse of children. The task force also recommended that in all cases of intrafamily violence, law enforcement personnel make arrest and prosecution decisions based on the nature of the offense, not the relationship between offender and victim.

Legislation expanding victim rights continues to be passed at both the state and federal levels. In one state in 1983, over one hundred bills concerning the rights of crime victims were introduced into the state legislature. At least five hundred bills were introduced into state legislatures throughout the country addressing the same issue. This legislative activity has included many bills establishing rights for crime victims for the first time.

Crime Victim Organizations

Victims of crime are far better off today than they were only ten years ago. Not only are there more services and professionals working at the local level to assist crime victims but legislation has been passed to guarantee them certain rights. On the national level and in every state, the plight of the crime victim has been presented to the legislatures, the courts, and the public. Two presidential commissions and many state investigatory bodies have published fact-finding reports, many of which have led to changes in the way in which the government responds to the needs of crime victims.

These achievements did not occur accidentally. Domestic violence shelters and rape crisis centers have established coalitions to coordinate state-level activities on behalf of victims of these specific crimes. In some of the larger urban areas, both formal and informal networks of victim service providers have been created to address local needs.

A number of different national organizations have been instrumental in focusing public interest and attention on the needs of crime victims. These groups have different agendas and different priorities, however, in the aggregate, they describe the broad range of crime victim interests throughout the country. While it is impossible to recognize even most of the local victim organizations that have worked to ensure better treatment of crime victims, some of the national organizations include:

American Bar Association (ABA) Victims Committee, which has published a number of booklets describing victim needs and has developed model legislation that guarantees certain rights to crime victims.

Mothers Against Drunk Driving (MADD), an organization started by the mother of a young girl killed by a drunk driver, that works for passage of stricter laws and sanctions against those people who are arrested for driving while intoxicated.

National Coalition Against Domestic Violence, which, as the name implies, represents the interests of domestic violence shelters, state coalitions, and service providers, and which supports legislative action to improve the extent and quality of services for victims of domestic violence.

National Coalition Against Sexual Assault (NCASA), which works to improve the treatment and services for victims of sexual assault through the over six hundred organizations nationwide that provide services to such victims.

National Organization for Victim Assistance (NOVA), which serves as a clearinghouse for victim information and which has been instrumental in establishing presidential and gubernatorial recognition of Victims' Rights Week.

Parents of Murdered Children (POMC), which provides services through local chapters to people who survive the violent death of a person close to them and which works to increase society's awareness of the problems of homicide survivors.

Society's League Against Molesters (SLAM), which works to prevent incidents of child abuse and molestation through stricter laws dealing with molesters and an employer's right to discover criminal records of employees.

Students Against Drunk Driving (SADD), which, like MADD, works to prevent incidents of drunk driving, but which does so by encouraging people not to drink and drive.

Sunny von Bulow National Victim Advocacy Center works to promote the responsiveness of the judicial system to the rights and needs of crime victims, and establishes programs to heighten citizens' collective consciousness concerning the plight of victims. The center maintains an extensive data base on state legislation that affects victims' rights and on third-party litigation.

Victims Assistance Legal Organization (VALOR), which serves as a clearinghouse for lawyers representing victims of crime, and works to achieve procedural changes to assist victims in lawsuits against third parties and others.

Washington Legal Foundation, which represents victims of crime in selected cases and also works to achieve legislative changes to help victims of crime.

Other national organizations have made important contributions to improve services to crime victims, and at least three associations of criminal justice professionals have been instrumental in similar efforts. The International Association of Chiefs of Police, the National District Attorneys Association, and the National Sheriffs Association have published books, reports, and monographs focusing on the plight of the crime victim. The National District Attorneys Association has been particularly important in this effort because most victim/witness service providers are employed by district attorneys.

All victim advocates and the organizations they represent deserve credit for the dramatic changes that have occurred in the courts and legislatures focused on improving the rights of victims of crime. In the next few years, these rights should increase in number and quality as society improves its services to crime victims.

Victims of Crime: Future Directions

In 1983, after approximately two hundred years of decisions, the Supreme Court of the United States, for the first time, recognized the rights of victims of crime. The court stated that the rights of crime victims are not guaranteed by the Constitution, but nonetheless should not be ignored. In the case before the court, which involved the conviction of a defendant for rape and sodomy, the victim's rights had been properly considered by the trial court when it refused to reschedule the case when the public defender the defendant wanted was unavailable but an equally competent public defender was available.

Recently, other courts have recognized the emerging legal rights of crime victims. Legal scholars have written law review articles on this topic.

However, crime victims do not have the same or even similar rights as those accused of crimes, and therein lies a problem for the future direction of the victims' movement. In broad outline form, there are two schools of thought about the best way to ensure fair treatment of crime victims. One believes the most effective way to help crime victims is to reduce crime through tougher criminal justice standards and longer prison terms. Victims will enjoy greater protection and more rights by removing or taking away rights from those accused of crime.

The other school believes that it is both impractical and politically unwise to take away the rights of those accused of crime. Rather, victim advocates should work to ensure better services and more compassionate treatment for crime victims.

Although occasionally there is a happy marriage of these essentially competing views, many victim advocates find themselves advocating one theory over another, and almost inevitably one seems to dominate the other. For instance, the Presidential Task Force on Victims of Crime made scores of recommendations to increase services for crime victims, but relatively few to take away the rights of the accused. However, one recommendation, the limitation of the Exclusionary Rule whereby illegally seized evidence may not be used in court for any purpose, dominated press reports about the task force and led to some organized opposition to the entire report.

An even better example concerns the issue of capital punishment. It is difficult, although not impossible, to find a relationship between victims' rights and capital punishment for the accused. Obviously, capital punishment is the supreme act of retribution, and that may be important for a few victims. However, capital punishment has nothing to do with providing better services for victims, nor does it address how society can treat such victims more compassionately. Nevertheless, many victim advocates support capital punishment and view it as a victims' issue.

During the next few years, victim advocates must increase their efforts in state legislatures and in Congress. Already, there is some backlash: during the last legislative term, three state legislatures refused to appropriate funds for existing crime victim compensation programs. Legislative gains are easily lost, and victim advocates may discover that affecting change in our society on a permanent basis requires not only the passage of appropriate legislation but also some vigilance to make sure it remains intact.

However, the courts appear to be the place where the legal rights of crime victims can achieve new directions. Coordinated efforts by victim advocates at the state and national level will be needed to identify "test cases" that can be brought to increase crime victims' rights. Whether through private prosecutions, third-party litigation, or some other court procedure, crime victims are likely to make the most progress during the next several years through the courts.

This book began with the description of a sexual assault victim I met, and how that chance meeting changed my view of the criminal justice system. During the past ten years, there have been significant changes; at least in most states, these victims enjoy a place in the criminal justice system, and their rights are recognized and, for the most part, respected.

We have a long way to go, however, for we need an even greater national concern and agenda for the establishment of legal rights for crime victims. When you have ignored a legitimate social concern for over two hundred years—as we have with crime victims—you do not change or improve the concern on a permanent basis in only a few years. All of us—particularly crime victims—should work for that national agenda. If we are successful, the next book about the legal rights of crime victims will be much longer.